Routledge Revivals

A Primer of National Finance

Originally published in 1919, *A primer of National Finance* discusses elements of financial principles with reference to facts and figures of British national finance, Britain's financial position and general outline of where finances stood at the time of publication. Higgs aims to explain essential information about the political economy in a simple and concise way to reach a wider audience on issues related to wealth and production. This title will be of interest to students of Economics and Political History.

A Primer of National Finance

Henry Higgs

Routledge
Taylor & Francis Group

First published in 1919
by Methuen & Co. Ltd

This edition first published in 2016 by Routledge
2 Park Square, Milton Park, Abingdon, Oxon, OX14 4RN
and by Routledge
711 Third Avenue, New York, NY 10017

Routledge is an imprint of the Taylor & Francis Group, an informa business

© 1919 Henry Higgs

Publisher's Note
The publisher has gone to great lengths to ensure the quality of this
reprint but points out that some imperfections in the original copies may
be apparent.

Disclaimer
The publisher has made every effort to trace copyright holders and
welcomes correspondence from those they have been unable to contact.

A Library of Congress record exists under LC control number: 20003419

ISBN 13: 978-1-138-19411-3 (hbk)
ISBN 13: 978-1-315-63899-7 (ebk)

A PRIMER OF
NATIONAL FINANCE

BY

HENRY HIGGS, C.B.

METHUEN & CO. LTD.
36 ESSEX STREET W.C.
LONDON

First Published in 1919

PREFACE

PROFESSOR BASTABLE concludes the Preface to the third edition of his well-known volume on Public Finance with the words: " A better-informed and more reasonable public opinion is an essential prerequisite of financial as of all other reforms in the modern State."

In many and not unimportant particulars of finance there is not yet agreement even among experts as to what is a reasonable opinion. The first qualification for forming such an opinion is a knowledge of the facts.

This primer is intended for those who have not previously given any attention to the subject. It will fulfil its purpose if it enables them to understand the annual Budget speech of the Chancellor of the Exchequer, and if it encourages them to read every year a full report of the Budget. Those who do so are not unlikely to feel a desire for further knowledge, and a note for their assistance is added at the end of the volume.

H. H.

July, 1919.

v

CONTENTS

A PRIMER OF
NATIONAL FINANCE

I

INTRODUCTORY

FINANCE deals with money matters and their management. It may be *Public* or *Private*—Public when it has to do with the finance of Government, and Private when it refers to that of individuals or groups of persons other than Government. Public and Private Finance have important effects upon each other, but are easily distinguished. What we pay to Government, for example, belongs to Public Finance. What we do with the rest of our money is a question of Private Finance.

It is well to begin with this distinction, and to keep it always in mind, because it shows us the folly of acting as if Government were a fairy godmother, able to endow us with all kinds of good gifts without our paying for them. Government can only spend what it takes from us, and this is limited by the capacity, and (in a country

like ours) by the consent, of the people at large
to pay taxes.

Public Finance, in so far as it refers to Governments in general and the principles upon which
good finance is founded, is sometimes described
as the Science of Finance. The thorough study
of this science requires a good knowledge of
economic theory, a sound training in the use of
statistics, an acquaintance with financial history
and financial literature, and with so much of law
and public administration as is necessary to
understand fiscal legislation and constitutional
law and practice, specially in their bearing upon
financial control. The subject is so vast that
Professor Jeze of Paris is preparing twelve bulky
volumes upon it. His elementary treatise alone
consists of over 1,100 large octavo pages. A
lifetime is required to master the history and
literature of Finance, the ideas, systems, methods,
and expedients of the past and present, the facts
and figures relating to the revenue, expenditure,
debt, currency, etc., of our own and other countries. All that is attempted in this little book
is to give some help to those who wish to understand the main facts of our own finance as it
now is.

Even in this limited field we must make a
further distinction between *National Finance,*

which relates to the Central or Supreme Government, and *Local Finance*, which relates to local or subordinate governments like County and County Borough Councils, Corporations, Urban and Rural District Councils, and Parish Councils. We shall be concerned mainly with the National Finance of the United Kingdom, but shall find it necessary to touch briefly upon the general principles of finance and upon Local Finance.

Finance is one of the most important of the duties of Government. Government is in our country representative of the people, who elect the members of the House of Commons. Upon this election depends the question what persons are to form the Government. A Government which does not command the confidence of the electors cannot long remain in office, but must give place to a new Government which has the support of the people.

It is, therefore, highly desirable that every citizen who wishes to do his duty to his country should know as much of financial matters as will enable him to follow the financial actions or proposals of Government, and that when a question arises or a discussion takes place as to the spending of public money or changes of taxation, he should be able to understand what it is all about and to cast an intelligent vote upon

the subject. Apart from this collective interest
which we should all feel in the welfare of the
community, we have a personal and individual
stake at issue. The Central Government of the
United Kingdom in the last year before the War
spent nearly 200 millions, and the local governments rather more. Statisticians are agreed that
in this way the people of the country paid about
one-sixth of their total income in rates and taxes.
In other words, they were free to spend ten
months of their actual incomes, but were called
upon to hand over the other two months' income
to be used on their behalf by the constituted
authorities. It is not suggested that so large a
proportion was contributed by all alike. The
wealthy paid more—in some cases very much
more—than one-sixth of their income, and the
poorest members of society paid less; but on the
average throughout the country the result was
as stated. In return for this contribution very
useful services were rendered to the people,
and if the money was all wisely spent we have
had value for it just as much as, and probably
much more than, if we had been left to spend
it at our own choice. But if you were asked to
surrender one-sixth of all you receive to a committee of persons who proposed to spend it for
your benefit, it is hardly conceivable that you
would take no interest in their proceedings.

You would desire to know what they were doing with the money: whether they were spending it for purposes of which you disapproved, or, if you approved of the purpose, whether they were spending more than was necessary to obtain the results you desired; whether the same results could be secured at less expense or better results at the same expense; and whether they were neglecting to lay out money upon necessary or urgent services, and practising a false economy to your ultimate detriment. Government is the steward of the public. A man who does not keep an eye upon the financial operations of his steward has only himself to thank if his pocket does not suffer from waste, inefficiency, or neglect. And every one of us is affected in pocket by National Finance.

The matter is put in a much stronger light if we take into account the fact that people have to live before they can pay taxes, and that the cost of living has first to be met. The total income of the country before the War, if divided equally between all the inhabitants, men, women, and children, would have been about 3s. a day. If we allow 2s. of this for housing, food, clothes, fuel, and other necessary expenses, what may be called the free income would average only 1s. a head. And if 6d. a day, or one-sixth of the total income, is paid to Government, this amounts to one-half of our free income. The cost of Government will be much higher after the War, and it follows that unless the total free income of the country is increased to a corresponding extent, either by increased production or by a lower cost of living, the pressure of taxation will be greatly intensified.

Many people appear to think that Finance is so dry and difficult, so complicated and technical, that they had better not bother their heads about it, but leave it, like the command of the Grand Fleet, to those whose business it is to understand and attend to it. This is a great mistake. Ignorance of financial matters does not produce indifference, or mean that we leave a free hand to Government. On the contrary, while failing to keep Government up to the mark in efficiency, it seriously hampers its action. Is new taxation proposed ? The man in the street sees no harm in it so long as it falls upon other people, though it may in the long-run recoil upon himself. But as soon as it touches his own pocket he finds objections and difficulties; and if the proposal, however good in itself, is sufficiently unpopular because it is not understood, Government is obliged to abandon it. Robespierre, one of the leaders of the French Revolution, protested vigorously against the idea that the purest part of humanity (which from his point of view was the poorest part of humanity) should suffer the humiliation of being denied the privilege of contributing its share towards the needs of the country. An ill-informed electorate is in danger of suffering not only this humiliation, but the material loss which follows upon a failure to carry out, for lack of funds, some measure which would be highly beneficial to the country at large. People are generally ready with reasons why they should not be called upon to pay more taxes. They will say that they already pay more than their fair share, though they have never studied the question of what is fairness in taxation. Or they will take refuge in such statements as " Government is wasting a great deal of money. If it would only stop this waste it would have enough without asking for more. Let it first make a good use of what it has got." The assertion may or may not be well founded, but it comes with an ill grace from those who have no idea how much Government spends upon its different services, and who would be puzzled to say in what direction it should economise. The great French writer M. Leroy-Beaulieu says that there are some sciences so lofty and serene that they leave in peace those who know nothing about them. Finance is not one of this number. Neither is it a mere affair of tact and intuition, but of severe science and erudition, and has a terrible fashion of avenging itself upon individuals and Governments which ignore or defy it.

Statesmen and officials have been too much accustomed in the past to think of finance as a matter merely of paying the Government's way from day to day and from year to year, and of raising taxation in such amounts and by such methods as will not arouse too much opposition among the public or among the supporters of the Government. It is now beginning to be seen that the real touchstone of good finance is the question whether it tends to promote or to injure the wealth and happiness of the country. The wealth must be produced before the financier can make use of it, and in a poor country good finance can only make the best of a bad job. But the richest of countries may be reduced to poverty by bad finance injuring the sources of wealth. There are in round numbers 13 millions of men who are Parliamentary electors, and to these have recently been added about $8\frac{1}{2}$ millions of women electors, making a total of $21\frac{1}{2}$ millions, as compared with less than $8\frac{1}{2}$ millions a year ago. The need for diffusing an elementary knowledge of the finances of the country, and sound views as to the amount and the justice of taxation, was never so pressing as at the present time. Our taxation has for many years been so small in comparison with our wealth that no great ability has been needed to enable the Government to pay its way. But the future has in store for us problems of a more serious character, and it will require all our wisdom and patriotism to find the best solution. The better our citizens are instructed the easier it will be for Government to manage our money matters in the best interest of the country.

If, on the other hand, the great masses of the people who have the power to make and unmake Governments are so ignorant of finance as to press Government to do ever more and more—which means increased expense—while, at the same time, they reject any proposal to increase their own share of taxation, the result will sooner or later be calamitous, not only to Government and to finance, but to the country at large.

In order to carry on its business Government must spend money, or incur *Expenditure*. To meet this necessity it must have an income, or *Revenue*. If the revenue is not sufficient to meet the expenditure—as usually happens in case of great emergency like a costly war—it can only make both ends meet by borrowing, or running into *Debt*. We have here three great divisions of our subject. Various economic questions arise out of these three topics, which we will examine in turn, first pausing to offer some general remarks upon financial statistics.

II

FINANCIAL STATISTICS

WHEN we enter into the details of National Finance we require the use of *Statistics*, which may be defined as organised figures. The first figures which we need in studying the financial position of an individual, a company, a corporation, or a Government, are an account of Income and Expenditure, and a statement of Assets and Liabilities. Our national accounts show the amounts received and paid by Government, and give some information as to its assets and liabilities. But as we shall see this is a good deal short of what is wanted to comply with the requirements of a properly constructed balance-sheet.

The most convenient summary of financial statistics for our purpose is the annual Statistical Abstract for the United Kingdom. It begins with a table of Imperial Revenue and Expenditure of the United Kingdom, the word " Imperial " being used because Local Finance is not included in the figures. Such statistics as we shall need will be found in an Appendix at the end of this volume.

Our national finance has been so violently disturbed by the Great War that the figures during the War are wholly abnormal. The details of these figures have not been fully published, and it will be convenient to select for explanation by way of example those of the last year before the War. The financial year begins on the 1st of April, and therefore runs into two calendar years. The usual practice is to refer to " the year ending the 31st March, 1914," or " the financial year 1913–14," but I propose throughout to describe the financial year by the single date of the year in which it begins and in which the greater portion of it falls. Instead of 1913–14, I shall therefore say 1913.

We start, then, with the figures for 1913:

Revenue.	Expenditure.	Surplus.
£198,242,897	£197,492,969	£749,928.

In a later table the aggregate gross liabilities of the State are shown as £707,654,110, and the estimated assets as £38,279,578, on the 31st of March, 1914.

The first point to be noticed is that the figure of Revenue is not the true Income of the year,

but is the revenue received into the *Exchequer*—
i.e., into the Accounts kept for Government
under that name at the Bank of England and the
Bank of Ireland—between the opening of the
Banks on the 1st of April, 1913, and their closing
at 4 p.m. on the 31st of March, 1914. It is
hardly necessary to explain to anyone who keeps
a banking account that in any year income
proper to the year is one thing and payments into
the Bank another, usually very different, thing.
The Revenue so paid in is not even the actual
Revenue collected in the year. In his Budget
speech in 1893 Sir W. Harcourt thought it
necessary to say: " I should like to state to the
Committee what, perhaps, everyone is not fami-
liar with—the distinction between Exchequer
Receipts and *Net Receipts*. The Exchequer
Receipts are the sums which the Exchequer
receives in the course of the year, and the Exchequer may receive some money belonging to
last year. But if honourable Members wish to
ascertain the yield of taxes they must take the
net receipts, and examine what is the actual
amount of taxation which properly belongs to
each year." We may supplement this by explaining that, as the Revenue Departments collect their receipts all over the country, a certain
time is occupied in remitting the revenue to

headquarters. The Departments pay in their revenue to the Exchequer in round sums day by day, and the total amount collected by their officers during the year is only ascertainable after the close of the year, when the accounts of the local offices have been examined. The taxes actually collected within the year include arrears of previous years, but from the total or gross receipts is deducted the amount of tax refunded, etc., within the year. The balance or net receipt necessarily differs somewhat from the payments into the Exchequer in the same year. While, on the one hand, as Sir W. Harcourt points out, the Exchequer receives money belonging to last year, it has not yet received all the money belonging to (and actually collected in) the current year. If these amounts were nearly equal, the account would not be much affected, but the variations in both directions are considerable. The revenue is paid in sooner or later, and if there is underpayment in some years, there is in other years a larger payment to the Exchequer than the net receipts for the year. But these fluctuations exert a distinctly disturbing effect upon comparisons—a short payment of a million in one year compensated in the following year producing a variation of double its amount when we make a comparison between the two years.

The term Net Receipts must not mislead us into thinking that the cost of collection is deducted from the gross receipts. All that is meant is that certain allowances, repayments, drawback of duties, etc., are subtracted from the gross receipts to arrive at the amount due to the Exchequer as net receipts from the taxes.

The broad principle is that all revenue must be paid into the Exchequer and all the expense of Government paid out of the Exchequer, and not out of the receipts. There are, however, some moneys which form an exception to this rule. They are said to be appropriated in aid of votes, and are known as *Appropriations in Aid*. Examples are fees paid by suitors; fines and costs recovered; fees for admission to Museums, Art Galleries, the Tower of London, etc.; fees paid for inmates of the Naval College at Osborne, of the military colleges at Sandhurst and Woolwich, and of reformatory schools; fees on admission to honours and dignities; fees for passports, proceeds of rents, sales of timber and old materials, the proceeds of work of prisoners, licences to put chairs in the parks or to open refreshment kiosks, harbour dues, payments for searches and copies of the records of births, marriages, deaths, and wills, sales of maps, Blue-books, and Government publications generally, advertisements in the *London* and *Dublin Gazettes*, and a great number of miscellaneous items. There are also contributions from overseas for repayments to the Army and Navy. The amounts so appropriated in aid in 1913 were—for the Army, £3,724,294; for the Navy, £2,086,528; for the Civil Service and Revenue Departments, £3,143,245—in all, £8,954,067, or in round figures 9 millions. In addition to this must be noted the payments made by the Woods, Forests, and Land Revenues for surveys, repairs, etc., and for costs of collection of rent and other revenues. These amount to about £190,000 a year, and are paid out of receipts. If all these appropriations had been paid in to the Exchequer, the revenue for 1913, instead of £198,242,000, would have been £207,386,000.

The precise nature of an Appropriation in Aid may be made clear by an example. If we suppose that I have a salary which is received monthly, and I pay this into my bank and draw cheques against my account in favour of various tradesmen, my bank-book reveals my income and expenditure to that extent. But if I receive various small cheques for literary work and change these cheques at my club, using the proceeds for petty expenses, my bank account will not contain any entry either of the receipt or expenditure of these amounts. I have appropriated them in aid of my petty cash; but they do not figure in my pass book either as receipts into or issues out of my account at the bank.

The propriety of intercepting receipts on their way to the Exchequer and appropriating them to meet expenses has been much discussed. They are mentioned here only to make clear their effect upon our financial statistics.

Yet another disturbing influence in the figures showing the receipts as apart from the true income of the year is found either in delayed clearances or in forestalments of dutiable articles. As the end of the year approaches, the returns published weekly in the *London Gazette* of Exchequer receipts and payments throw before them the shadow of a probable surplus or deficit. If there is likely to be a substantial surplus and a probable reduction of the income tax, experience points to the probability of a simultaneous reduction of duty upon beer or spirits, tea or tobacco. In that event merchants delay the clearance and payment of duty upon new stocks until the Budget proposals have been adopted. Conversely, any expectation of increased duty leads to their taking as much as possible out of the warehouses before the increased duty comes into effect. The true revenue of the year as it would be if based upon consumption is thus obscured, and the real figures are best obtained by taking an average over a longer period—say for three years. It is possible for the authorities after the event—and, indeed, in a very short time after the event—to put a figure upon the abnormal clearances, and to estimate the amount of revenue which has been gained or lost to a particular year by the precautionary measures of the merchants. But unless such a figure happens to be mentioned in the Budget statement, it is not available, until of late years supplied in the Reports of the Revenue Departments which appear long after the close of the year.

Without entering into further detail we may say briefly that some of the revenue proper to the year has been used to meet expenses without passing into the Exchequer account; that some of the Exchequer receipts are arrears due in former years, but not collected in the proper year, or, if collected, not fully paid in; and that various sums due to the Exchequer for the year are still outstanding.

We have so far been considering only the Revenue receipts, but a good deal of other money comes into the Exchequer account. Money is borrowed by Government for longer or shorter periods, and recoveries are made of money

2

which has been advanced by Government, so
that the Exchequer really received in 1913 about
£45 m.* more than the revenue proper, and
on the other side of the account £42 m. was
issued out of the Exchequer over and above
the expenditure chargeable against the revenue.
These "other Exchequer issues" were mainly
for capital purposes—advances, repayments of
borrowed monies, Sinking Fund, etc. Expenditure
is defined as issues out of the Exchequer exclusive
of expenditure not chargeable against Revenue—
that is, exclusive of the "other Exchequer
issues" to which we have just referred. Here,
again, we must note that our £197 m., though
issued from the Exchequer, was not all spent.
A certain amount of money was in the hands of
various financial officials who need working
balances with which to carry on, and some money
had been paid out to authorities like the Road
Board and to special accounts not closed at the
end of the year. In a word, the issues from the
Exchequer are not the true expenditure of the
year. The account is a cash account, or a receipts

* The symbol "m." is used to represent a million.
Mr. Gladstone was accustomed in his memoranda to use
"m." for thousands and m̄ for millions. In the present
magnitude of our national finance thousands may usually
be neglected in a general survey.

and payments account, and not an income and expenditure account.

A cash account, or even an income and expenditure account, is evidently incomplete without a capital account or statement of debt and assets outstanding. Our information upon this subject is meagre. The Aggregate Gross Liabilities of the State on the 31st of March, 1914, were £707,654,110. The Estimated Assets are shown as Suez Canal Shares, estimated market value £34,929,000, and Other Assets £3,350,578 —a total of £38,279,578. We will examine these figures in greater detail later. The Exchequer Balances at the Banks of England and Ireland were £10,434,519 at the end of 1913, and £6,329,160 on the 31st of March, 1913.

The gross capital liabilities are in respect of borrowed money, funded and unfunded debt, terminable annuities, etc., and do not include liabilities to trade creditors, to service pensioners, and others. The assets of Government are, of course, enormously more valuable than £38 m. Some years ago a Member of the House of Commons complained of the amount of our National Debt. Other countries in Europe had, he admitted, larger debts. But he urged that these had been incurred partly in order to nationalise railways, lay out extensive forests, and construct industrial and other works productive of Government revenue, and so alleviating the debt burden. " What," he asked, " have we to show for our National Debt ? " The retort was instantly forthcoming: " We have the British Empire to show for it ! " There is much force in this. The outlying parts of the Empire are of great direct and indirect material help to the people in these islands. But although in the War they have nobly assisted us both with men and treasure, they do not ordinarily contribute directly to our national Exchequer. The British Empire is not an asset which can be capitalised in a balance sheet, and we cannot put a figure even upon the " goodwill " which it represents to the Mother Country.

At one of its first meetings, over fifty years ago, the International Congress of Statistics, composed largely of eminent officials, expressed a desire that there should be compiled for each country a Tableau de la Fortune de l'Etat, or Schedule of State Properties. But the aspiration has not been fulfilled. The labour in a country like ours would be considerable, and the valuation would offer many practical difficulties. But there seems no good reason why we should not have some information—even though it be of a summary and approximate kind—as to the value of land, buildings, etc., which are the property of the nation. The Public Accounts Committee has called attention to the fact that there is not even a proper inventory, to say nothing of valuation, of the articles in our great national museums. No figures are available as to the total value of ships, stores, machinery, plant, and other Government property. The Post Office does indeed publish a Capital Account, from which it appears that in 1914 the property held by the Post Office was valued at about £14 m. The lands, etc., held by the War Department alone —camps, barracks, parade, recreation, and manœuvre grounds, artillery and rifle ranges, factories, etc.—are of very great value. The Government buildings and their sites in London are worth many millions, and even in foreign countries we have valuable sites and buildings for diplomatic and consular purposes. The valuation of such properties as fortifications and naval yards would not be an easy matter. But as Government pays to local authorities a contribution of nearly a million and a half annually in lieu of rates upon a great deal of national property, and as Government itself assesses those properties for that purpose, there is in existence a considerable nucleus of information which might easily be made available as far as it goes.

In 1833 a Return was ordered to be presented to the French Chambers shewing the buildings belonging to Government and set apart for the public service. National palaces and the properties of local authorities were not included, and many buildings were entered without any attempt to set a value on them, or were valued at a nominal figure. The schedule contained 8,778 properties, and the values added up to about 536 millions of francs—a ludicrously small figure in the circumstances. In 1876 a more serious effort was made in a Table of State Properties printed in two large volumes. This time properties in the Colonies and in foreign countries were included, but the properties of local government, railways, schools, religious edifices, national monuments, roads, canals, rights of foreshore, riparian rights, and many other Government properties, were omitted. The result was—(a) Properties affected to the public service, 17,899, of the estimated value of 1,948 millions of francs; (b) properties not affected to the public service, 9,098, of the estimated value of 1,650 millions. The second category consisted mainly of woods and forests and vacant lands. Taken together, we have about 3,600 millions of francs.

M. Leroy-Beaulieu, from whom these figures

are quoted, estimated the whole National Domain of France in 1906 at 15,000 millions of francs—a figure which he says will be more than doubled when—about the middle of this century—the railways fall in to the State. Now, 1,200 millions sterling is a respectable fortune in State capital. What sort of figure would be arrived at by an inventory of our own State fortune it is impossible to say. But we had evidently a great deal more than 38 millions of assets to show for our National Debt in 1913.

The point of importance for our present purpose is not merely that without a capital account for each Department of Government we are unable to allow for the interest which forms part of its true cost, but that, be the absolute value of State property what it may, changes occur in the course of the year in respect of certain assets, and that these changes, which are not revealed in the accounts, may be misleading. If a Department starts the year with a great accumulation of stores which is seriously depleted at the end of the year, the amount paid out for new stores is a false guide to the cost of its operations. On the other hand, a great addition to its stores would inflate its expenditure in the year, but not its expenditure for the service of the year. In short, there is no proper capital account to complete our national balance-sheet and to answer the crucial question of the real cost of Government.

A scientific and systematic basis of public accounting and the presentation of clear and complete financial statements are essentials of good financial administration; and as the pressure of taxation increases, as the franchise extends and education improves, the public may be expected to be more and more interested in the large and increasing part of their money which is taken from them to be spent by Government. Accounts which convey a true and precise impression not only satisfy curiosity up to a point, but stimulate further interest; and where financial intelligence is well diffused the problems which arise are more easily solved. People who are uninformed or whose information is inaccurate and confused cannot sympathise with difficulties which they fail to understand. In the absence of right impressions they are almost certain to form wrong ones, and instead of co-operating towards the best solution of financial difficulties there is grave danger of their obstructing it, to the injury of society and themselves. This is true of all classes, whether they object to necessary taxation, or, while approving of its purpose, object to its falling upon themselves, or whether they fail to object to it when they ought to do so. In his Budget speech of 1860 Mr. Gladstone said: " It was, I think, Lord Londonderry who complained of the people of England as exhibiting an ignorant impatience of taxation; but I think were he to rise from the dead and again take his place in this House, he would be very much more likely to describe them as distinguished by an ignorant patience of taxation." It is, however, altogether too indiscriminate to regard taxation in itself as an evil to be combated or a blessing to be welcomed. Whether we do well or ill to be impatient depends upon what we are impatient about, and it is here that ignorance is to be deplored. The first step to dispel ignorance in financial matters is to publish the facts and figures in a proper form. They are even then liable to be misunderstood and mis-used by inexpert persons, but this makes it all the more necessary that they should be rendered as intelligible as possible, and that they should be supplemented by such notes and warnings as will safeguard a careful reader against serious pitfalls.

The Exchequer account includes both current and capital expenditure, both current and capital receipts. In current expenditure is included provision for the purchase of sites and for the erection of buildings, unless the amount is so large as to disturb seriously the finances of the year. In that case an Act is usually passed to authorise borrowing. The Land Registry (New Buildings) Act, 1900, for example, authorised the issue of £265,000 out of the Consolidated Fund, to be raised by terminable annuities for such period not exceeding fifty years as the Treasury may fix. The cost which figures in the course of a year is thus one year's annuity. Similar provision has often been made for Army and Navy works, the Post Office telephones and railway, and for large schemes of public buildings generally.

Returning for a moment to the Revenue side of the Exchequer account, we find Estate Duties, which in some cases represent the whole amount due in respect of the estate of a deceased person, in other cases an annual instalment, where the executors have elected to spread the payment over nine years, paying interest on the arrears. The amount of instalments not yet paid varies from year to year. In this, as in the former example, the account of receipts and expenditure is, as it were, fortuitously put upon a different basis from what it would be if the whole expenditure were brought into account when it occurs and the whole duty paid at once.

The question whether the national accounts

should be presented upon a cash basis (Receipts and Payments) or upon a basis of " accruals " (Income and Expenditure) has been much debated. Those who desire to follow the arguments used on both sides may refer to the authorities mentioned in my lectures on National Economy, and to the Seventh Report of the Select Committee on National Expenditure. Taking our accounts as they stand, and admitting such advantages of promptitude and facility as are claimed for them, it would still seem desirable that they should be supplemented at a later date than the closing of the present account by some memoranda and figures which would give us a closer approach to a full and accurate picture of the finance of the year. The documents presented to Parliament in 1913 relative to finance are more than fifty in number, and the figures contained in these documents are not always in harmony with each other or with the Statistical Abstract, although the causes for the discrepancy are frequently not stated. An important step in reform would be the issue once a year of an authoritative balance-sheet of the last year, with a memorandum giving all the essential information upon both sides of the account, with approximate figures when exactitude is impossible, as in the estimated amount of arrears of taxes.

A statement of public revenue and expenditure from the Exchequer account, which was formerly published only once a quarter, was ordered by Mr. Lowe to be printed weekly in the *London Gazette* on and from the 16th of February, 1870, and this enables the public to follow its banking account and to note the state of balances in the Exchequer. But it is a long way from this to understanding the inwardness of the figures as an indication of our financial position. " The mere figures of the comparison between one year and another," said Mr. Gladstone in 1863, " invariably require to undergo much careful analysis before they can become the basis of sound conclusions," but the material which is essential for such an analysis is not supplied.

If it is difficult to compare the figures of one year with those for its predecessor, the difficulty is enhanced when the comparison is over a term of years. Not only are changes made from time to time in the basis and classification of the figures, but the value of money may have undergone serious changes—a fact to which Mr. Gladstone himself was not always alive. In his Budget speech of 1863 he pointed out that in ten years from 1842 to 1852 the taxable income of the country had increased by 6 per cent., and in eight years from 1853 to 1861 had again increased by 20 per cent. "That," he said, "is a fact so singular and striking as to seem almost incredible. [Sir John Pakington: " Australia !"] Australia ! Oh no ! . . . My right hon. friend is evidently lost in the depths of heresy." Now, it is a mere matter of history and statistics that, as might have been expected from economic reasoning, the Australian gold discoveries were followed by a serious fall in the value of gold—in other words, by a rise of prices. In the ten years from 1842 to 1852 the level of prices fell from 115 to 100. From 1852 to 1861 it rose by 20 per cent. A readjustment of values under such conditions leaves, of course, many incomes nominally unchanged. But the stimulating effect upon trade and industry of a steady, continuous rise of prices is undoubted. The profits liable to income tax tend to show at least an equivalent rise to the range of prices. A nominal increase of 20 per cent. in taxable income is in effect no real increase at all when prices generally have risen by 20 per cent., and the " heresy " was on the side of Mr. Gladstone.

Financial statistics, like all other statistics, need careful and intelligent handling. It is easy to compare one figure with another, but we must know what the figures stand for and what they mean before we can be sure that we are

observing the golden rule of comparing like with
like. How many persons, for example, ever
give a thought to the difference in fiscal time
between one year and another ? To quote again
from Mr. Gladstone (1861): "The revenue of
this country is in the gross about £200,000 a day
for every paying day in the year; and that part
of it which depends strictly upon operations from
day to day may be stated at fully £100,000 a day.
The year 1860–61 was, for every practical purpose,
shorter by three days than 1859–60. It was
shorter in this way: 1859–60 was a leap year,
which accounts for one day and 1860–61 was in
the predicament—most happy with reference to
our other interests, but not favourable to the
interests of the Revenue—of both commencing
and ending with a Sunday. By means of this
closing Sunday there was a loss of a clear day's
income on the balance-sheet. And the third day
is accounted for by the circumstance that in the
course of the year 1860–61 there fell two Good
Fridays; one of them was at the very close of
the year, and the effect of it, with the following
Sunday, was to throw some business and some
payment of duty forward into the account of the
following year." The deduction of these three
days, according to Mr. Gladstone, represented
revenue to the amount of £300,000, for which

he made allowance in order to arrive at " a fair and just comparison." Since 1861 we have not only a larger daily revenue, but the Easter holiday has been very generally extended from Good Friday to Easter Tuesday, and the effect of an Easter Monday falling on the 31st of March would on balance be considerable. Or again, if the last day of the financial year is a Sunday, and pensions or other periodical payments which would have been paid on that date are thrown forward to the next financial year, or if there are fifty-three days for the payment of weekly wages instead of fifty-two, there is a resulting disturbance in comparison. And such disturbances do not compensate one another. A national balance-sheet properly drawn would call attention to such points, and enable us to make some allowance for them.

Just before the War an American Commission visited this country to study our financial system. Their Report, published in 1917, contains a good deal of praise, but singles out as a serious defect the absence of a general consolidated statement of audited expenditure of the Government as a whole, not only by votes, but by individual services, and bringing together all expenditures for the same services or purposes if met partly from the Consolidated Fund Services and partly from the Supply Services. They say this "could easily be remedied did Parliament so desire. All that would be required would be—(1) The abolition of the system of appropriations in aid; (2) the removal of the inconsistencies now existing in the distribution of charges between the Consolidated Fund Services and the Supply Services; and (3) the requirement that the Comptroller and Auditor-General, in addition to submitting his technical reports on appropriation and other accounts, shall prepare and lay before Parliament a general report on the audited receipts and expenditures of the Government as a whole."

The object of this chapter is not to offer criticism upon our financial figures, but to warn the student against running into errors which are often made by those who do not understand with what precautions the figures must be read.

III

THE EXPENDITURE OF GOVERNMENT

THE amount which is spent by Government depends upon two factors—what Government does or attempts to do, and how it sets about it. The first of these is policy, and the second is administration. If no fault can be found either with the wisdom of policy or the efficiency of administration, then the expenditure is not open to criticism.

Opinions will always differ as to what Government ought and ought not to do, and what is (or even whether there is such a thing as) "the proper sphere of Government." Few people will dispute the statement that the object of Government is to promote the welfare of the people; but in pursuing its object of achieving the good of that portion of mankind which is within its jurisdiction, what are the limits of Government activity? To this question the Anarchist replies that Government is an evil, and that we should do better without it. Others accept it as for the time a necessary evil, to be kept within the narrowest limits, and to be ultimately stamped out as no longer necessary. Herbert Spencer, in his *Social Statics*, triumphantly asks: " Have we not shown that government is essentially immoral ? Does not it exist because crime exists, and must government not cease when crime ceases, for very lack of objects on which to perform its functions ?" M. Paul Janet, in his *Histoire de la Science politique*, says: " The object of government is to prepare men gradually for that perfect state of society in which law and government itself would become unnecessary." And Jules Simon says: " The State ought to render itself useless and to prepare for its own decease."

At the opposite extreme come those who desire that the functions of Government should be, not minimised, but maximised, and that Government should, to begin with, own all the land, capital, and productive resources of the country. Without entering into discussion of these views, we must recognise the fact that the advance of civilisation adds to the complexity of our needs and to the multiplicity of our desires, and that many things which are conducive to our health, security, and comfort, can be better assured by Government than by individual effort.

Communities, like individuals, develop new needs. What collective or Government action should be undertaken is affected by the existence, the consciousness, and the urgency of these needs, and must therefore vary from age to age and from country to country. Whether it is or is not desirable that Government should undertake a particular service depends so much upon the circumstances, that no absolute principle beyond that of expediency can be of practical service to us in this respect. Circumstances are always changing and policy must adjust itself to new conditions from time to time, and have regard to the present and prospective wealth of the country.

When the question has been settled what Government is to do—and it can do very little without expense—the amount which is spent is largely dependent upon the efficiency of administration. In public as in private life money may be wasted by setting about the right thing in the wrong way. Even if the method be good, its execution may be defective. The organisation of the public service and of its officials may be imperfect. The agents of Government may be incompetent or non-competent, lacking the special kind of knowledge or the special qualities needed for their particular business. Overlapping, undue elaboration, lifeless routine, ignorance, neglect, sometimes even a misguided zeal, are among the causes of waste and extravagance. What Government can undertake with fair prospects of success must depend very much upon the fitness of its servants. In this and other ways policy and administration react upon each other, but, taking these as we find them, we will consider the figures of Government expenditure in 1913.

Table C (Appendix) shows the Imperial Expenditure under its principal heads, as issued from the Exchequer.

The *Consolidated Fund Services* are fixed by permanent Acts of Parliament, unlike the *Supply Services* which are settled annually by Parliament.

The National Debt services amounted to 24½ m. They are discussed in Chapter V.

In 1913 no issue was made for the Development Fund, but some explanation of this Fund is necessary. It was established in 1909 under the control of the Treasury, and Development Commissioners were appointed to consider applications, made by bodies not trading for profit, for money for any purpose calculated to promote the economic development of the United Kingdom. The moneys are provided by Parliament, and are granted by the Treasury, upon the advice of the Commissioners, either as a gift or a loan. In 1913 the Commissioners recommended grants of £615,000 and loans of £152,000 for Agriculture and Fisheries, Forestry, Land Drainage and Reclamation, Rural Transport, Inland Navigation, etc. Receipts by way of repayment or profit are paid into the Fund, and the amount standing to its credit in cash and investments on the 31st of March, 1914, was over £2½ m. An account of the operations of the Commission is presented annually to Parliament.

The Road Improvement Fund, under a Road Board, was also set up in 1909. It received out of the Exchequer in 1913 the sum of £1,394,951. Of this, £789,703 came from the duties on motor spirits, £605,248 from carriage licences. The expenditure of the Board was £15,698 for administration, £16,950 grants for construction of new roads, £622,763 grants for improvements of roads, and £296,892 loans for improvements of roads, or £952,295 in all. The receipts include repayments of loan and interest on dividends, and the Board had thus improved its balance in hand by nearly half a million in the year—an example of the difference between Exchequer issues and true annual expenditure. The Exchequer was, moreover, in arrear in payment of the net proceeds of motor spirit duty and carriage licences. The amount due to the Board

in respect of 1913 was £1,434,711, and a sum of
£107,865 in arrear on 31st of March, 1913, had
become £147,625 a year later. In other words,
the Exchequer had still nearly £150,000 to pay
to the Board.

Payments to the Local Taxation Account,
£9,734,128. The figures are discussed in
Chapter VI.

The Civil List, now £470,000 a year, is fixed
by Act of Parliament on the accession of the
Sovereign, who surrenders his life interest in
Crown lands, which yielded in 1913 £530,000 net,
in return for a settled annuity. It would, however, be a great mistake to suppose that the whole
£470,000 is available for His Majesty's private use.
The charges upon it for salaries, works, Royal
bounty, etc., leave only £110,000 a year for Their
Majesties' Privy Purse. The pensions, salaries,
etc., charged on the Consolidated Fund are chiefly
those of persons whose independence is supposed
to be better secured by withdrawing their salaries
from the discussions of Parliament year by year
The Speaker, the Comptroller and Auditor-General
and his Assistant, and the Judges, including
County Court Judges, are paid in this way.

The *Consolidated Fund* is nothing more or less
than the amount standing to the credit of Government in the Exchequer Account; and when an

Act of Parliament directs that certain charges
are to be paid out of the Consolidated Fund, this
means that Government must find and pay the
money somehow without reference to the state
of business in Parliament. Where, on the other
hand, charges have to be paid out of " moneys
provided by Parliament," the House of Commons
must vote the money out of the Consolidated
Fund, and the payment cannot be made until
the money is voted. Parliament has at different
times granted perpetual or hereditary pensions
for real or supposed services to the nation. It
has entered into a bargain with the Sovereign for
an annual Civil List, and with the holders of the
National Debt for the payment of their interest,
and it is thought that nothing is gained by
bringing such matters, which cannot fairly be
set aside by one of the parties, under annual
discussion.

The grand total for the Consolidated Fund
Services is £37,322,969. The most economical
Government has no means of reducing these
charges—which, owing to the vast debt now
created, will amount for some time to a great
part of the annual expenditure—except by the
extinction of debt as opportunity offers. The
same thing is to a great extent true of the salaries
of permanent officials who have vested interests

in their appointments. To large amounts of expenditure upon contracts, leases, etc., Government is committed in advance, and cannot go back upon them, however much it may deplore the original decision to embark upon particular enterprises.

We turn now to the *Supply Services*, so called because they are voted annually in Committee of Supply in the House of Commons. We will enter into detail in the first item, Army Services, as an illustration.

The Appropriation Accounts made up at the end of the year, and audited by the Comptroller and Auditor-General, show the total amount expended and how it was divided between certain heads. The sum issued from the Exchequer for the Army amounted to £28,346,000. The actual gross expenditure was £32,090,397, met as to £3,724,295 by receipts or appropriations in aid, leaving a net expenditure of £28,366,102. The heads or divisions of net expenditure are—Pay, £8,457,378; Medical Establishments (including Pay, etc.), £446,819; Special Reserve, £687,084; Territorial Forces, £2,820,452; Military Education (Establishments for), £154,962; Quartering, Transport, and Remounts, £1,817,644; Supplies and Clothing, £4,576,343; Ordnance, £735,419; Armaments, Aviation, and Engineering Stores,

£1,809,343; Works and Buildings, £2,435,164; Miscellaneous Effective Services, £62,062; War Office, £442,284; Non-effective Pay (*i.e.* pensions, etc.) for Officers, £1,827,752; Ditto for Men, £1,950,487; Civil Ditto, £137,464; Balances irrecoverable and Claims abandoned, £5,445.

Before the money for the Army was voted an Estimate was laid before Parliament showing how much was required under each of these heads. The Appropriation Account reproduces these figures, shows the amount actually spent under each head, and gives an explanation of any considerable variation from the estimate. The account also states the amount appropriated in aid under each of the same heads. For the most part, the receipts are payments made by India, Egypt, and the overseas parts of the Empire for the services of British troops or materials supplied by the Army. A similar contribution is made for pension charges. Other receipts are derived from the sale of properties, cast animals, and articles no longer required, grazing rents on remount farms, purchases of discharge, stoppages for quarters, barrack damages, etc.

Parliament lays down every year a maximum number of men for the Army and the Navy. The total authorised for the Army in 1913 was 185,000. Deducting 3,036 permanent staff of the Territorial establishments, 1,151 for staff and departments, and 1,480 for miscellaneous services, the authorised regimental establishments were 179,933. The actual number never amounted in the year to 172,000 and was in some months below 167,000.

The Ordnance Factories Department spent about £3 m. in the year, but as it sells its products to the Army and Navy for such amounts as will cover its expenditure, it does not figure separately in the account of Exchequer issues. A nominal or token Vote is laid before Parliament to give an opportunity for discussion, and an account of its business is annually presented. Its capital in land, buildings, and machinery was valued at about £2½ m., and it had in hand cash, stores, and material of the value of over £2 m. on 31st March, 1914.

Separate accounts are also presented for the Army Clothing Factory, for Military Works out of borrowed money, for Chelsea Hospital, for the Military Savings Banks, and for the Finances of the Territorial Forces.

The issues for the Navy amounted to £48,833,000, the gross expenditure to £50,819,150, the appropriations in aid to £2,086,529, leaving a net actual expenditure of £48,732,621. The maximum number of men voted was 146,000.

Separate accounts are presented for Dockyard Expenses, the Victualling Yard, the Royal Naval Torpedo Factory, the Naval Savings Banks, and Greenwich Hospital.

The issues for Civil Services amounted to £53,901,000. The gross expenditure was £55,005,721, appropriations in aid £2,335,087, actual net expenditure £52,670,634. The issues for Revenue Departments £29,090,000, gross expenditure £29,460,754, appropriations in aid £808,158, actual net expenditure £28,652,596. The two services combined received £82,991,000 from the Exchequer, but spent only £81,323,230 of this amount. The apparent expenditure, as judged by Exchequer issues, is thus £1,667,770 greater than the real expenditure for the year.

Details of all Civil expenditure under 124 votes are given in the Appropriation Accounts as already described. The total issues for the Supply Services amounted to £160,170,000, and this, with the Consolidated Fund Services already referred to, amounted to a total of £197,492,969 chargeable against Revenue. But in addition to this must be taken into account issues out of the Exchequer to meet capital expenditure. Though there is no proper capital account of Government, there is some attempt, far from logical or complete, to treat certain capital expenditure specially. The amount is advanced out of the Exchequer as required, and is repaid by annual instalments spread over a number of years, the amounts being repaid in most cases by Votes of Parliament. It is hardly necessary to point out that in a properly drawn balance-sheet of the year's finance the effect of these capital operations would be clearly brought out. The total issues to meet capital expenditure were £4,220,749, exclusive of £380,000 worth of Exchequer Bonds issued to the National Telephone Company in part payment of the purchase money of their undertaking.

The expenditure for Civil Services is divided into a number of classes or blocks in the accounts. The classification is amended year by year by transfer of items from one class to another, and, as the amounts are sometimes considerable, there are serious pitfalls in comparing the classes from year to year. Within each class come numerous Votes for separate Services or Departments. And the detailed expenditure under each Vote and its subdivisions is set out in the Appropriation Accounts, which are audited and reported upon by the Comptroller and Auditor-General, whose report is referred by the House of Commons to a *Public Accounts Committee* which calls before it and questions witnesses from the Departments concerned as to any matters which arise out of the accounts where irregularity or waste is suspected.

The checks upon expenditure are numerous. The Treasury must approve the Estimate presented in detail to Parliament, and no increase of numbers or alteration of pay is valid without Treasury approval. Parliament must sanction the expenditure proposed in the Estimates before it can be incurred. The Auditor-General will question any payment unless it is duly authorised, is supported by proof of payment, and is charged to its proper head in the Accounts. Finally, the Public Accounts Committee, with the Auditor's Report before it, will follow up any question he has raised, or will raise one of its own, in the effort to discover any improper expenditure, though it is restricted from questioning matters of policy which do not arise out of the Accounts. The primary and ultimate responsibility for spending the country's money in such a way that full value is received for it rests upon the authorities of each Department. But everybody knows that all these precautions fall short of securing the desired result. It is sufficient for a small body of Members of Parliament, who are not experts in the matter, to be formed into a Committee to inquire into expenditure, and for them to scratch the surface, to discover irregularities of substance as distinct from the irregularities of form which are the primary concern of audit.

The Select Committee on National Expenditure in its Seventh Report (Form of Public Accounts), H.C. 98/18, points out that " the total cost of the Services for which they provide is not included either in Estimates or Accounts." " Except in the few cases where Departments compile manufacturing or commercial accounts, no Department can render an account of its expenditure, because no Department fully knows it. Its buildings, stationery, rates, pensions, postal, telegraph, and telephone expenses, are all finally recorded as matters of account in the accounts of the Departments administering those Services." A rough estimate is made every year of the amounts which are expected to be paid for services rendered to another Department, but except for this guess, and for some tables in the Appropriation Accounts, we are very much in the dark.

The published figures of Government expenditure show us how much money has been issued and under what heads. The accounts of the various Departments show how much has been paid out for salaries, for travelling, for stores, etc. But the question whether the money has been well spent cannot be answered from these details. The Select Committee concludes that the present form of Accounts and Estimates is "non-significant" and of little value for purposes of control. It is proposed that the Estimates and Accounts should, in future, be prepared on an income and expenditure basis, and that a beginning should be made forthwith with a new form of Army Estimates. The object aimed at is to show the actual cost of each Service, which, as we have seen, is not the same thing as its actual cash outlay, but will include the value of services rendered and stores utilised. Statistics will be prepared in greater detail of the cost of various divisions of Services, and, where possible, this will be reduced to a cost per unit. For example, the Royal Military Academy at Woolwich costs so much, has so many cadets, and the cost per cadet will be worked out, making it possible to compare the cost per unit one year with another, to compare the cost per cadet at Woolwich and at Sandhurst, etc. Similarly, the cost of the Hospital Service will be worked out at so much per day for occupied bed. Such statistics, intelligently handled, will enable useful comparisons to be made between one hospital and another and between Army and Navy or civilian hospitals. This change marks an important step forward

in scientific administration, and has in it the
germs of great reform. A more striking example
of the uses and, indeed, the necessity of statistics
as applied to public affairs could hardly be provided.

In studying the figures of national income,
national expenditure, and national trade, account must be taken of alterations in the value
of money as measured by the movements of prices.
The purchasing power of the pound sterling
varies considerably year by year, and sometimes
month by month. The Japanese Government
issues tables of trade and finance which contain
much interesting information, the value of which
is enhanced by an index number showing the
movement of prices. If, for example, the value
of certain exports has doubled since the outbreak
of war, and if we see at once that prices have
also doubled, we realise that the quantities
exported have remained about the same, and so
avoid a dangerous error. The index number of
the *Economist* before the War was at the end of
July, 1914, 116·6, taking as the basis the average
prices of 1901–1905 as 100. In other words,
prices had increased (prices of principal commodities wholesale) by one-sixth above the
average of the first five years of the century.
The index number at the end of August, 1918,

was 284·8—roughly speaking, two and a half times as high as before the War. In other words, a sovereign would then purchase only as much in the wholesale market as 8s. before the War. But even in peace time the movements of general prices must always be watched side by side with the movements of expenditure. The Consolidated Fund Services are very little affected, as the debt charge remains unaltered, and fixed salaries and pensions, the Civil List charges, and similar items, remain the same. Even in the Supply Services the pay of the naval and military forces and the Civil Services is not always supplemented by such a peace bonus as will meet a fall in the value of money. But where materials are concerned for building and arming ships, for machinery and stores, stationery, etc., an increase in prices must always be kept in mind. To take a simple example, assume that I spent £3 a year on stationery before the War and now spend £6. My expenditure on stationery is doubled. But assuming, further, that I use the same kind and quality of stationery, we must not conclude that I have used twice as much. If, in fact, the price has tripled, so that I now pay £6 for what would only have cost £2 before the War, I have actually diminished my consumption, which used to be half as much again in quantity

4

as it is now. Such allowances have seldom been
made by critics of Government expenditure.
It has moreover been too usual to regard the
quantity of expenditure rather than its quality.
The question, What are you getting for your
expenditure ? is one which goes to the very
roots of efficiency in public finance, and the
answer to it is one which demands a much
greater use of the statistical faculty than anything to which we have yet approached.

Parliament has attempted to control the
national expenditure by a series of steps—by
limiting the grant to the Crown; by setting up
an Exchequer control, requiring authority before
the grants were paid out; by earmarking the
grants to specific purposes; by instituting an
audit to ensure that the grants were applied to
their proper objects and were not exceeded;
by entrusting the Public Accounts Committee
with the duty of scrutinising the accounts and
the report of the auditor upon them; and has
tried the experiment of an Estimate Committee
to consider the demands of Departments before
the Estimates were voted. It is now proposed to
apply the principles of cost-accounting to the
Estimates so as to bring out the amount required per unit of service. Apart from all this,
there are questions and debates in Parliament,
and the efforts of the Treasury and of the Depart-

ments themselves to secure economy, and from time to time Parliament inquires into the details of some section of the public service by means of a Committee. But the control of expenditure will never be effective and complete until we have what is called an *Efficiency Audit*, which looks at results obtained and discovers when they were an unsatisfactory return for the money which has been spent. Such an inquiry, conducted by permanent experts who devote their whole energies to the work, should provide Parliament and the country with full and authentic information upon the merits of expenditure, as distinct from its legal and formal propriety. Dealing with the past and going upon accomplished facts and settled figures, it would put its finger upon waste and mismanagement, would enable safeguards to be taken against their recurrence, and would have a bracing and tonic effect upon public administration generally. Occasional, limited, and amateur inquiries into particular Services at particular times cannot be so effective as a permanent, continuous, independent, and all-embracing expert inquiry. Such a searchlight would not interfere with the operations of Departments, but it would reveal facts upon which Parliament and the proper authorities could take such action as might be required to secure value for the expenditure of Government.

IV

THE REVENUE OF GOVERNMENT

IT is sometimes said that the difference between private and public finance is that the individual must regulate his expenses by his income, but that Government has to adjust its revenue to its expenditure. This supposes that Government first decides how much it will spend, and then casts about for ways and means to make both ends meet. That this is not necessarily the case is seen from the experience of the United States. The revenue derived from its Customs tariff and other sources was for many years before the War sufficiently large to meet any probable expenditure, and was sometimes so much in excess as to cause embarrassment. The programme of expenditure was settled without any detailed reference to or correlation with the probable revenue, and was in no way adjusted to it except in so far as a sense of proportion restrained Congress from launching out into expenditure on such a scale as would have necessitated increasing the revenue. But even in our own country the expenditure is always limited to a great extent by similar considerations. The wealth of a country is limited; the amount of that wealth available for taxation is still more limited; and an eye must always be kept upon the point at which the inconvenience of increased taxation will outweigh the advantages of increased expenditure.

We will now examine the figures of revenue in 1913 (Appendix, B). First in order comes the Customs, which yielded to the Exchequer £35,450,000. The amount collected (net receipts) was £35,568,581. Excise contributed £39,590,000. Net receipts were £39,657,957. Customs duties are levied upon dutiable articles brought into or sent out of the country. The export duty on coal, repealed in 1907, was a Customs duty. Excise is collected from certain dutiable articles produced and consumed at home. Both sets of duties are under the management of one Board, the Commissioners of Customs and Excise, from whose Report the figures given on p. 54 are compiled.

NET RECEIPTS OF CUSTOMS DUTY FOR THE FINANCIAL
YEAR BEGINNING APRIL THE 1ST, 1913.

		£
Beer		31,643
Cocoa		341,489
Coffee and chicory		220,352
Dried fruit		513,601
Rum	2,585,691	
Brandy	1,183,830	
Total potable spirit		4,435,500
Sugar		3,272,044
Tea		6,498,816
Tobacco		18,263,479
Wine		1,152,291
Motor spirit		823,623
Other articles		15,743
		35,568,581

The duty on cigars amounted to £457,315
(included in tobacco).

NET RECEIPTS OF EXCISE DUTY FOR THE FINANCIAL
YEAR BEGINNING APRIL THE 1ST, 1913.

	£
Beer	13,622,971
Spirits	19,539,777
Railway duty	288,368
Glucose and saccharin	56,491
Patent medicines	360,377
Playing-cards	33,543
Liquor licences (including club duty and monopoly values)	4,516,679
Other licences	1,200,603
Other receipts	39,148
	39,657,957

Motor-car licences yielded £674,174 of the above. Liquor licences do not include the yield (over £400,000) of brewers' licences, which are included under the head of Beer.

Taking Customs and Excise together, it will be seen that alcoholic drink produced nearly 43½ m., tobacco 18¼ m., tea, coffee, and cocoa over 7 m., sugar 3¼ m.—in all 72 out of 75 m.

When an article liable to Customs duty is imported and the duty has been paid, it is said to be " cleared," and passes out of the Customs control. But large quantities of imports get no further than the docks, whence they are shipped again to foreign countries. Arrangements are made under which such articles may, under Customs supervision, be deposited in a *Bonded Warehouse*, the owners entering into a bond to pay the Customs duties upon the goods if they pass into internal consumption. No duty is paid if the articles are re-exported from the bonded warehouse. Or, again, an article which has paid duty may be exported either in its original form or after it has been worked up, and in such cases a *Drawback* or repayment in respect of the duty received may be allowed. Finally, we must note that certain allowances are made in respect of bonded articles to compensate for loss of quantity while they are in bond—*e.g.*, for evaporation of spirits, leakages, bottling of wines and spirits, the roasting of coffee, the mixing of tea, etc. The quantities imported differ from " the quantities which are retained for home consumption," partly because of re-exports and partly because of this loss in bond.

The quantities (ooo's omitted) retained for home consumption in the *calendar* year 1913, and the average consumption per head of population, were as follows:

			Per head.
Beer	..	34,988 barrels,	or 27·36 gall.
Cocoa	..	78,273 lb.	,, 1·70 lb.
Coffee and chicory	..	319 cwt.	,, 0·78 lb.
Currants	..	1,243 cwt.	,, 3·03 lb.
Raisins ..	..	725 cwt.	,, 1·76 lb.
Rum	..	3,320 proof gall.	,, 0·07 gall.
Brandy	..	1,504 proof gall.	,, 0·03 gall.
Total potable spirit imported	..	5,629 proof gall.	,, 0·12 gall.
Spirits home made	..	26,163 proof gall.	,, 0·57 gall.
Sugar	..	33,918 cwt.	,,82·52 lb.
Molasses and glucose	..	3,943 cwt.	,, 9·60 lb.
Tea	..	305,489 lb.	,, 6·64 lb.
Tobacco	..	96,110 lb.	,, 2·09 lb.
Wine	..	11,367 gall.	,, 0·25 gall.

Figures of consumption " per head of population " are not of much absolute significance in the case of alcohol and tobacco, of which the consumption is mainly confined to adult males, but, assuming the age-distribution and the habits of consumption to remain the same, they are serviceable for comparisons.

The Customs tariff begins with the words: " Beer of the descriptions called Mum, Spruce or Black Beer, and Berlin White Beer, and other preparations, whether fermented or not fermented, of a character similar to Mum, Spruce, or Black Beer," etc.—a typical example of the jargon which disfigures our legislation. Mr. Gladstone once asked the Revenue authorities what Mum is, but they were unable to discover. Some statutory distinction is needed between herb beers, ginger-beer, and other so-called beers, and those which are of sufficient alcoholic strength to come within the duty, but it does not appear that any useful purpose is served by the perpetuation of an enumeration not understood even by the Revenue officers.

The beer which pays Customs duty is, of course, imported or foreign beer, and the amount collected is very small compared with the yield of Excise on home-made beer. The taxation of chicory would not by itself be worth while, but for the fact that it is frequently mixed with coffee. The revenue from cocoa and coffee could not be abandoned without seriously affecting the revenue from tea, which is much more considerable. When one article is a substitute for another, or what economists call a "rival commodity," a tax upon one necessitates, for obvious reasons, a tax upon the other. The taxation of sugar, therefore, leads to the taxation of molasses, glucose, and saccharin.

A curious feature in the revenue from dried fruits is that apricots, if dried, crystallised, or glacé, are charged as plums; but if imported in pulp or tinned or bottled in syrup or water, are charged as sugar in respect of the fruit, while the syrup is charged with its proper duty unless the merchant chooses to pay duty on the whole weight at the fruit rate. All other dutiable fruit in syrup or water is charged the fruit duty on its weight of fruit without squeezing out the syrup or water, and the syrup is separately charged. The merchant may, if he chooses, pay on the whole weight at the fruit rate. It follows that apricots alone of all fruits may be charged as sugar, while some syrup is charged, not as sugar, but as fruit. The net effect upon the true figures is not stated, but is probably inconsiderable. Railway duty has steadily diminished, about 19 per cent. in the ten years 1903 to 1913, owing mainly to the gradual abolition of second-class fares, the duty applying only to passenger fares exceeding one penny per mile. It does not extend to Ireland. The rate of duty is 2 per cent. on urban traffic and 5 per cent. on other traffic.

The " Other Licences " are for appraisers and house agents, auctioneers, hawkers, makers or vendors of patent medicines, motor-spirit dealers, pawnbrokers, plate-dealers, keepers of refreshment houses, tobacco manufacturers and dealers; the so-called *Establishment Licences* for male servants, motor carriages and cars, Hackney carriages (including motors), and armorial bearings; gun licences, game licences, game dealers, and dogs. The total amount paid by the public in respect of these " Other Licences " was nearly 3 millions; but, as we shall see in Chapter VI., the proceeds were largely devoted to Local Finance. (See also Appendix, Table C, note, p. 154.)

Estate duties, Exchequer receipts, £27,359,000 (net receipts £27,165,123). Details are given in the Report of the Commissioners of Inland Revenue. In round figures 21½ m. were received from Estate duty, 4½ m. from Legacy duty, and £900,000 from Succession duty. As Corporations never die, a duty of 5 per cent. is levied yearly on the net annual value, income, or profits, of all their real or personal property liable to duty. The amount produced in 1913 was a little over £59,000.

The gross capital of which the Commissioners had notice in 1913 as passing at death amounted to £327,701,824 gross and (after deduction of debts, etc.) £296,432,158 net. In addition, are estates exempt from duty as not exceeding £100 net value, amounting to £1,768,928. Of the Estate duty, 18½ m. were in respect of personal and 3 m. of real property. The capital paying Succession duty was about 29 m.

Stamps (exclusive of Fee and Patent stamps) paid into the Exchequer, £9,966,000. The net receipts were £9,983,363, made up as follows (000's omitted):

	£
Deeds, bonds, contract notes (above 1d. duty) Foreign certificates and share warrants ..	5,603
Companies' capital duty and loan capital duty	726
Bills of exchange, bankers' notes, and compotion for duty on bills and notes	1,160
Life and marine insurances	300
Receipts, drafts, and other penny stamps ..	2,016
Licences and certificates	175
	9,983

The net receipts from Land Tax were £690,007. £700,000 was paid into the Exchequer. The tax does not extend to Ireland. The aggregate of the unredeemed Quotas, or annual liabilities, to Land Tax on the 25th of March, 1914, was £929,208. Remissions are made annually to owners with small incomes, and £2,273 was written off as being charged on Government property.

Inhabited House duty: Net receipts, £1,994,400; payment into the Exchequer, £2,000,000.

Property and Income Tax: Payment to Exchequer,£47,249,000; net receipts,£47,240,771. (000's omitted.)

	£
Schedule A. Ownership of lands, houses, etc. ..	10,304
Schedule B. Occupations of lands, etc. (mainly farmers' profits)	214
Schedule C. Profits from British, Indian, Colonial and Foreign Government securities	2,867
Schedule D. Business, professions, and employments except E	27,293
Schedule E. Salaries of Government, Corporation, and public company officials ..	3,223
Super Tax	3,339
	£47,240

The total gross income brought under review was in 1913 £1,111,456,413. Allowing for exemptions for income under £160, charities, hospitals, friendly societies, etc., foreign dividends belonging to foreign residents, allowances for repairs to lands and houses, empty property, wear and tear of machinery or plant, and other reductions, the taxable income was £907,151,813. From this were abated £133,195,066 under the graduated scale, £12,518,938 on life insurance premiums, and £5,860,262 relief in respect of children. The total income on which tax was received was therefore £755,577,547.

Land Value Duties: £715,000 paid into the Exchequer; net receipts, £734,893, of which (000's omitted)—

			£
Increment Value Duty	..	..	34
Reversion Duty ..	..	..	80
Undeveloped Land Duty	..	..	274
Mineral Rights Duty	..	..	345
			734

The Postal Service contribution to the Exchequer, £20,300,000, compares with net receipts of £21,220,105. The Telegraph Service Exchequer payment, £3,100,000; net receipts, £3,071,170. Telephone Service Exchequer payment, £5,775,000; net receipts, £6,563,316.

Crown Lands (net receipts): £530,000 paid to Exchequer; gross receipts, £730,319. Amount due to Exchequer after deducting expenses (see p. 15), £543,658.

Receipts from Suez Canal Shares and Sundry Loans, £1,579,972, is made up as follows (000's omitted):

				£
Suez Canal shares dividends	..	..	..	1,246
Cunard Steamship Company, interest on advances	.. .. ..	..	..	53
Greek Loan, 1832, repayment	..	..	..	11
Fiji grant in aid, further in part repayment			..	5
Gold Coast, repayment of advances		..	..	20
Liberian Government	..	..	..	3
Persian Loan repayment ..	..	..	..	10
Northern Nigeria repayment	..	..	..	205
Uganda Railway repayment	..	..	..	12
British East African Protectorate, interest			..	11
Nyasaland, interest	..	..	..	1
				£1,579

The Miscellaneous Revenue paid into the Exchequer was £1,078,000 from Fee and Patent stamps and £1,225,925 receipts by Civil Departments, etc.

The net receipts for Fee and Patent stamps were £1,084,203. The great bulk of the stamps is for legal business, but over £100,000 was received for company registration and over £60,000 for district audit. The Patent stamps yielded £335,349.

The Miscellaneous Revenue received in cash comprised £800,675 from the Mint, being the excess of its receipts over and above the amount appropriated to meet its expenses for the year; £187,047 paid by the Bank of England mainly out of profits of its note issue: interest on deposit funds invested by the Paymaster-General, £12,610; £15,000 in respect of escheated estates; and various small sums received by public Departments and not appropriated in aid.

The grand total of Exchequer Revenue is thus £198,242,897. Of this, Customs and Excise account for £75 millions; Income Tax, Estate Duty, Taxes on land and houses, and stamps (excluding Fee and Patent stamps), for £88 m. Fee and Patent stamps another million; Posts, Telegraphs, and Telephones, £32 m.; Crown Lands half a million; Suez Canal Shares over a million;

the Mint and the Bank of England another million. The division in the accounts is intended to suggest that only £163 m. is in the nature of taxation, the remaining £35¼ m. consisting chiefly of special payments by the public for special services (Posts, Telegraphs, Telephones, Crown Lands, etc.), sometimes described in Government Returns as " non-tax revenue."

A caution must again be given here against extracting figures from a work of reference, even though it be so good and authoritative as the Statistical Abstract, and using them as a basis of deduction, and especially for comparisons, without first understanding how the figures are arrived at and what they really mean. The Reports of the Revenue authorities contain much excellent statistical material and sometimes illuminating comment for which we should look elsewhere in vain. Thus we learn, for example, that in comparing the Customs and Excise revenue for 1913 with that of the year before we must make allowance for abnormal features accounting for £3½ m. The great national coal strike in the spring of 1912 checked the consumption of the chief dutiable articles, and the revenue of 1912 further suffered by postponed clearances of tea, sugar, and tobacco at the end of that year. On the other hand, the revenue of 1913 profited not only by this postponement, which was made good when the Budget was announced, but by forestalments or abnormal clearances at the end of 1913 in anticipation of increased taxation, especially on alcoholic drinks. In this way the revenue of 1913 included some of the revenue on articles which would normally have paid duty in 1912 and in 1914. The figures given are—Spirits, £1,367,000; Beer, £428,000; Wine, £42,000; Tea, £347,000; Sugar, £220,000; and Tobacco, £1,010,000. If revenue from consumption were taken it would be more nearly uniform. The revenue paid differed considerably from the true revenue belonging to each year. A hot and dry summer in 1913 stimulated, as usual, the consumption of beer; a cold and wet winter stimulates the consumption of spirits.

We have already seen that the expenditure is elaborately accounted for. First we are told how much is required for each service, and, so far as the Supply Services are concerned, how much is estimated or forecast as the probable expenditure for each Department under a number of subdivisions. The accounts show the actual expenditure in the same detail, with explanations of differences between the estimated and the actual expenditure. We have nothing comparable to this in regard to revenue. In many

5

countries the Budget figures of revenue are stated in detail, and not merely in bulk, and at the end of the year it is possible to see where the revenue has exceeded or fallen short of the forecast, and to learn the reason why the yield of revenue was not in accordance with expectation.

Taking merely the instances mentioned above, a report upon the Finance of 1913 would show that the Exchequer issues differed considerably from the real expenditure, as in the case of the Road Board, to which nearly £1,200,000 was issued, though it spent less than half this amount and lent a sum of less than £300,000. The Exchequer receipts from the three great Revenue Departments were £2 m. less than the net receipts. How far the assets of Government were increased by the purchase of lands, buildings, increased stores, etc., out of revenue, or decreased by sales treated as revenue, etc., and the figures of income tax, death duties, etc., in arrear at the beginning and end of the year, would be stated, with other information which is essential to an understanding of the true change in our financial position.

It has been seen that the great bulk of our revenue is derived from taxation. We cannot here enter into discussion of what are called the principles of taxation. The revenue must be sufficient, but it is of the highest importance that it should be raised by methods which are not injurious to the ultimate interests of the country and that the amount to be raised should be fairly adjusted as between different classes of taxpayers. It is now generally agreed that fairness requires a larger proportion of their incomes to be taken from the richer than from the poorer classes. If Government required 20 per cent. of the national income and taxed everybody at that rate, it is evident that the man earning 30s. a week would be harder hit than the man whose income is £30 a week, who could spare £6 a week much more easily than the labourer could spare 6s. Admitting this principle it can only be carried out satisfactorily if we have trustworthy information as to the amount of, and the distribution of, the wealth of the country. Until we know how many people fall into each group in the scale of wealth, and how much is contributed by each group in the taxation, we can only grope after an approach to justice. What is called *direct taxation*, like the income tax, is paid once for all by the person from whom it is collected, and the tax is not passed on to another person. *Indirect taxation*, like the Customs duties on tea and tobacco, is first paid by the importer, but is passed on by him to the merchant who buys from him, and so on from one dealer to another until we come to the final purchaser. Even here a question arises whether the duty on, for example, the tea, sugar, and beer which their employers supply to domestic servants is borne by these servants or by their masters. And some of the problems of the effects of taxation, usually called its *incidence*, are of the greatest difficulty, depending largely, as they do, upon questions of fact not easily ascertained as to the bargaining powers of the parties to take advantage of any rise or fall in the taxes. As indirect taxes cannot be graduated with reference to the wealth of the taxpayer, it follows that taxes upon articles of general consumption like tea, tobacco, sugar, and beer, press more severely upon the less wealthy sections of the community.

Before the War the German Empire, like the United States, relied mainly upon Customs duties for its revenue. Some German economists and politicians not only denounced this arrangement because of its effect upon the prices of articles of general consumption, but went so far as to assert that since Government was the greatest purchaser of stores of all kind, and since the increased cost of living necessitated higher wages and salaries to the army of officials, the Government really derived no financial benefit from the Customs tariff, the expenditure of Government being increased, as they maintained, by at least the amount of the Customs revenue.

The supporters of indirect taxation, apart from those who desire it as a protection of native industry, point out that so long as large numbers of people are exempt from income tax and contribute little or nothing to death duties, it is only by indirect taxation that some assistance to the cost of Government is derived from them. It is also claimed that such taxes are optional in the sense that people who do not choose to smoke tobacco or drink alcohol escape taxation upon these articles. Some writers urge that indirect taxation is of a relatively painless character, the tax being concealed in the price of the article. Others insist that this is a condemnation of the tax; that taxation ought to be open and evident, and that the taxpayer should realise the fact and the amount of taxation when he pays it. The ultimate effect of privation is the same in either case. It is also objected that indirect taxation takes more out of the pocket of the consumer than finds its way into the Exchequer, seeing that each dealer adds some percentage of profit to what he pays for an article, and the original tax charge grows with each transaction of purchase and sale. A change in the income tax is less disturbing both to the operations of trade and commerce and to the cost of collection than a change in indirect taxation, and, finally, indirect taxation adds to the difficulties of ascertaining and adjusting the effects of taxation upon different classes. The administrative difficulties attendant upon the collection of income tax from people of small incomes appear less serious since the National Insurance scheme of collection by stamps affixed by the employer has come into operation.

Direct taxation is not without its critics, and the income tax is roundly abused for its lack of simplicity, the irritation and waste of time which results from controversy over its application, and from numbers of anomalies and unfair features. The Income Tax Act of 1918, a consolidation of existing law and practice, extends to 190 pages. An expert lawyer, financier, and accountant would be needed to understand it. A Royal Commission is now sitting to consider the income tax in all its aspects, and to report what reforms are desirable.

It was for a long time, and until recent years, a superstition of British finance that the yield

of direct and indirect taxation should be approximately equal, and a raising or lowering of the one
was accompanied by a corresponding movement
of the other. The following figures have been
given to Parliament on behalf of Government:
In 1903–04 indirect taxation produced 50·7 per
cent. of the revenue, and direct taxation 49·3
per cent. In 1913–14 indirect taxation accounted
for 42·5 per cent. of the total. In 1918–19 it
yielded only 30·21 per cent., (or 18·63 if we include
the figures of excess profits duty). Taxation
per head of population is stated to have been
£3 10s. in 1913–14, and £16 12s. 10d. in
1918–19, of which £10 5s. 2d. came from direct
taxation.

What proportion direct taxation should bear
to indirect taxation cannot be determined by
any such simple rule of thumb as is mentioned
above. Those who pay direct also pay indirect
taxation, and everything depends upon the
articles selected for indirect taxation and upon
the distribution of wealth throughout the community. There is undoubtedly a growing
opinion in favour of direct taxation in all wealthy
countries. Indirect taxes are not always very
elastic, as increased prices resulting from higher
taxation tend to check consumption—markedly
so in the case of alcoholic liquors. The elasticity

of direct taxation was formerly regarded as an incentive to Government expenditure, since the money is raised, as it were, by a stroke of the pen. It may, however, be pushed to a point at which it discourages production and saving, in which case it is not only ineffective in its object, but is a serious menace to the national welfare. At what point the income tax should begin, so as to avoid trenching upon the margin of bare subsistence, and by what steps it should be increased or graduated, are questions upon which statistics may afford much guidance; but a number of other considerations have to be taken into account. Professor Bowley has recently analysed the division of the product of industry before the War. He gives the total income of the people from home sources as from £2,000 to £2,100 millions in 1913. Of this, more than half was earned by those who were exempt from income tax as having an income of less than £160 a year. Allowing for payments to Old Age Pensioners and for receipts from small properties, the owners of which fall below the £160 limit, nearly 60 per cent. of the national produce was in the hands of the non-income-tax-paying group. The 1,100,000 income-tax payers and their families received about £742 m. of the national income, and after allowing for their subsistence—

the average family being taken at 4½ persons—
the maximum income open to additional taxation
before the War is estimated to have been about
£300 m. This may seem a startling conclusion
when it is remembered that during the War
the taxation was actually increased by £459 m.
in 1918 as compared with 1913. But it must
always be remembered that prices had more
than doubled.

Statistical analysis of this kind gives us some
rough idea of the distribution of income and
taxation. But perhaps enough has been said
to show that the percentages of direct and
indirect taxation do not take us very far in the
direction of deciding how far the present revenue
system is a fair one. The question how steep
the graduation of taxation ought to be, or, in
other words, by what steps and by what degrees
taxation should increase in proportion with
higher incomes, is very far from being settled.
Mr. Herbert Samuel discusses the taxation of the
various classes of the people in his Presidential
Address of this year to the Royal Statistical
Society. From the report in the Society's Journal
of March last I extract his conclusions as to the
percentages of income paid in taxation by
families of two adults and three children, but
the whole address should be studied:

Income.	Earned Income.			Unearned Income.		
£	1903.	1913.	1918.	1903.	1913.	1918.
50	9·1	8·7	—	9·1	8·7	—
100	6·2	6·0	13·8	6·2	6·0	13·8
150	5·0	4·9	11·0	5·0	4·9	11·0
200	5·6	4·8	10·3	7·8	7·0	12·4
500	6·6	5·8	13·1	8·8	9·9	18·1
1,000	7·4	6·6	19·4	10·3	12·2	26·5
2,000	6·6	5·8	25·6	9·8	12·0	33·6
5,000	5·6	6·8	37·2	9·6	12·4	43·5
10,000	5·1	8·1	42·6	9·5	15·1	50·3
20,000	4·9	8·3	47·6	10·0	16·0	58·1
50,000	4·8	8·4	50·6	10·2	18·1	63·9

He also sets out the percentages of income contributed in each class from direct and indirect taxation respectively. In 1913 his figure for the family with an income of £100 is 6·0 per cent., for indirect taxation and nothing for direct taxation. In 1918 the figure 6 becomes 13·8. At the other end of the scale the £50,000 family paid 0·08 indirect tax in 1913 and 0·1 in 1918. Towards direct taxation such a family paid 8·4 per cent. on earned income in direct taxation in 1913 and 50·6 per cent. in 1918. A similar family paid 18·1 per cent. on unearned income in direct taxation in 1913 and 63·9 per cent. in 1918.

The effect of the War upon the distribution of

taxation has been a revolution of a very drastic character. The figures do not, of course, include local taxation. In an emergency so severe the State must take the money where it is to be found, and it would be futile to impose heavy taxation upon those who have not the means to pay it. Mr. Rowntree estimated the human needs of labour at the prices of July, 1914, to cost 35s. 3d. a week for a man with a family of three young children if they were to be adequately fed and decently clad, and put the figure at 20s. for a single woman. At present prices he alters the figures to 75s. 9d. and 43s. a week. Facts like these must be borne in mind in considering the capacity of the poorer classes to bear taxation.

V

NATIONAL DEBT

THE gross liabilities of the State (what we generally call the National Debt) amounted on the 31st of March, 1913, to £716,288,421, and a year later to £707,654,110. The debt is due mainly to war. In 1899 it was only £635 m. Four years later, after the Transvaal War, it exceeded £798 m. It was steadily reduced in the next eleven years by £91 m., but has now, thanks to the Great War, soared into figures of astronomical magnitude.

We will take for analysis the pre-War figure at the end of 1913. This was made up as follows:

				£
Funded debt (nominal amount)	..	..	..	586,717,872
Estimated capital liability in respect of				
terminable annuities	..	..	..	29,552,219
Unfunded debt	..	..	..	35,000,000
Other capital liabilities	..	..	..	56,384,019
				£707,654,110

The *Funded Debt* was originally so-called because it was charged or secured upon a particular fund, such as the proceeds of a particular branch of revenue. It has now come to mean a debt incurred for an indefinite period, and is sometimes called *permanent* debt as distinguished from *floating* or *unfunded* debt, which is intended to be of short duration—for a few months or, at most, a few years, repayable at a fixed date.

The nominal amount of the debt is the amount which Government has promised to repay. If we suppose a Government to issue a loan of £10 m. at 5 per cent., at the issue price of 98, and if the loan is fully subscribed, it receives only £9,800,000, but undertakes to pay £10 m. when the loan is redeemed. If in course of time the market price falls to 96, Government might purchase £100 of its own stock for £96, and by cancelling the stock diminish its nominal debt by £100; but this does not affect the liability of Government to pay a full £100 in case of compulsory redemption as against a holder who is unwilling to take less.

Terminable Annuities are annual payments for a limited period, for life or for a fixed number of years. If I purchase from the National Debt Commissioners an annuity for life, or say for fifteen years certain, and pay £1,000 for the annuity, the Commissioners will apply the

£1,000 to the redemption of debt, and will pay
me the agreed annuity until it expires—*i.e.*, on
my death in the first case or at the end of fifteen
years in the second. When the annuity comes
to an end the transaction is closed. The Commissioners have exchanged a temporary or
terminable annuity for the right to a perpetual
annuity. They have paid year by year at a
higher rate than if my £1,000 had remained part
of the debt, but they pay for a shorter period.
Their liabilities at any moment in respect of
these annuities depend upon the ages of the life
annuitants at the time, the number, amount,
and conditions of the various annuities, and the
market rate of interest. Apart, therefore, from
the cessation or the shortening of the term of old
annuities and the creation of new ones, the
actuarial value of the present value of the
annuities varies from year to year.

Terminable annuities may be created in favour
of Government Departments like Savings Banks
or Courts of Justice, which, having dormant
balances, deposit with the Commissioners for
cancellation a quantity of Government stock
on condition that an annuity is paid for a certain
number of years. The transaction amounts to
an investment on the part of the depositors, who
receive, so to speak, their annual interest and

in addition a payment which is an instalment of return of capital. Of the £29½ m. which we have in view, almost exactly one-half was in respect of annuities held by private persons.

The Unfunded Debt consisted as to £20½ m, of Exchequer Bonds, repayable in April, 1915. and as to £14½ m. of Treasury Bills, repayable six months from date of issue.

The " Other Capital Liabilities " represent the outstanding liability to the Commissioners in respect of various loans authorised by Parliament, to be repaid by annual instalments. In many cases the repayments are made by an annual vote of Parliament. The effect is to spread the cost of some large capital operation, like the building of Government offices or the construction of the Pacific cable, over a number of years. The debt is thus gradually extinguished almost from the time of its creation. These other capital liabilities are, like the unfunded debt, excluded from the total of *dead-weight* or permanent debt. Naval and Military Works account for £25½ m., Telegraphs and Telephones for £21 m., of the total £56 m. under " Other Capital Liabilities."

It is good policy to keep the debt as small as possible, and in times of peace two Sinking Funds are in operation for this purpose. The first of these is the *Old Sinking Fund*, and consists

of any surplus of Exchequer revenue over the
issues out of the Exchequer for the year chargeable against revenue, the last column of Table A
in the Appendix. Unless Parliament otherwise
determines, this is handed over after the end
of the year to the National Debt Commissioners
for the reduction of debt. The *New Sinking Fund*
is arrived at by providing every year as a charge
against the revenue a fixed amount (£24½ m.
in 1913) for the service of the debt. This fixed
sum is higher than the estimated amount required,
and the excess over and above the payment of
interest, annuities, and cost of management,
is applied to the redemption of debt. If no new
debt is created, this procedure provides a con-
stantly increasing balance available every year,
the balance obviously increasing as the debt
charges diminish.

Apart from the sinking funds and the terminable annuities there are some other resources,
not considerable in amount, applied to the
redemption of debt. Examples are sums paid for
redemptions of land tax, or compositions for
stamp duty which give freedom from future
payment. The revenue of the year is not entitled
to benefit by the whole amount of lump sums
of this character at the expense of the revenue
of future years. In the same way Suez Canal
shares belonging to Government may be drawn

and paid off, and the proceeds are devoted to debt redemption. So also certain windfalls to the Exchequer, such as the receipts from the Chinese indemnity and occasional donations and bequests.

We are now in a position to examine the operations of the National Debt Commissioners in 1913. They began the year with a funded debt of about £593½ m., of which about £4 m. was entitled to interest at 2¾ per cent.; and the remainder to 2½ per cent. Taking first the fixed provision of £24½ m., we find it accounted for as follows:

	£
Interest on funded debt	14,787,109
Terminable annuities	3,202,026
Interest on unfunded debt ..	1,115,850
Management of the debt	166,530
New Sinking Fund	5,228,485
	£24,500,000

The Sinking Fund moneys applicable to redemption of debt in any year are not always fully applied within the year. The Commissioners do not always effect their purchases of stock, etc., immediately on receipt of the money. The balance of cash in their hands at the end of the year is applied in the following year. The full consideration money for the Debt created in one year may not be received

6

by them till after the close of that year. The
reduction of the funded debt by various means
was as under:

	£
Conversion into annuities	972,710
Redemption of land tax and compositions for stamp duty	413,448
New Sinking Fund 1912–13 (part)	4,229,219
,, ,, ,, 1913–14 (part)	325,000
Received on account of China indemnity ..	756,607
Sundry minor receipts	39,001
	£6,735,985

The Funded Debt was thus reduced from
£593,453,857 to £586,717,872.

The capital liability in respect of Terminable
Annuities was reduced by £1,967,689, taking
into account the annuities expired or reduced in
their duration and those newly created. On the
other hand, other Capital Liabilities increased by
£1,569,363. Allowing for £1,500,000 paid off
from Unfunded Debt, the total debt redemption
for the year amounted to £8,634,311, agreeing
with the opening sentence of this chapter. The
amount of nominal debt actually redeemed does
not agree with the cash available for that purpose,
since the cash will purchase a larger amount of
stock standing below par. The Sinking Funds
are, of course, suspended during a time when
we have to borrow large amounts instead of
being able to pay off debt.

If we were discussing the growth of our debt or comparing it with the debts of other countries, we should have to attend to many considerations which are frequently left out of sight. Firstly, we must take account of the whole debt, national and local, since local government has a wider sphere at one time than another, or in one country than another. Secondly, the sphere even of these united Governments varies. One Government may spend a great deal and another very little upon such a matter as Public Health. In some cases railways, tramways, electric light and gas undertakings, waterworks, and even (as in the United States) telegraphs and telephones, may be left to private enterprise, and in others may be operated by central or local government. Thirdly, the assets held against the debt differ. Fourthly, account must be taken of the growth of population and of wealth, the numbers and fortunes of the people in the community. Fifthly, changes in the value of money are to be noted and allowed for. Sixthly, the rate of interest or annual cost of the debt is to be considered. And, lastly, it is of some importance how far the debt is held within the country and how far it is an external debt, though the consequences of this difference are often stated in terms which are exaggerated and indefensible. Proposals have recently been made for heroic measures to wipe

off the whole or a large part of the National Debt
by an enormous levy on capital. All these
questions are of great economic importance and
require highly skilled statistical treatment.
Without attempting to discuss them here, it may
be stated that various estimates of our national
wealth agree in fixing the figure of £15,000 m.
as the minimum value of the capital wealth of the
United Kingdom in 1913.

The Estimated Assets, which, according to the
official return, "admit of being calculated,"
amounted on the 31st of March, 1914, to
£34,929,000 estimated value of Suez Canal
shares; £190,000 advanced for the purchase of
bullion for coinage, to be repaid by the Mint;
£46,044 lent to the Government of the East Africa
Protectorate; £1,294,534 due from the Colonies
as their contribution to capital expenditure on the
Pacific cable; £1,820,000, nominal value of the
debenture stock of the Cunard Steamship Company, held as security for the repayment of advances made to the Company under an Act of
1904; total, £38,279,578. To this may be added
the balances in the Exchequer—£10,434,000.
The true assets of Government are a matter of
conjecture. Mr. Pethick Lawrence has estimated
them at £600 m. in 1914. At the present moment
they are immensely larger.

VI

LOCAL FINANCE

LOCAL GOVERNMENT is a subdivision of Government, entrusted with the local administration of certain local affairs through local officials. Its powers and duties are regulated by the central or supreme Government. Some functions formerly discharged by the central Government have been transferred to Local Government. To meet its expenses it is provided with the power of levying rates upon the occupiers of land and houses within its jurisdiction. The value of these properties is assessed, and a rate is fixed annually at so much in the £ upon the assessed value. Other resources are contributions from the central Government, receipts from various undertakings for the supply of water, light, tramway and other services, etc.

The total receipts of local authorities in the United Kingdom in 1913 amounted to £200,057,768, the total expenditure to

£200,080,692, and their debt on 31st of March, 1914, to £654,969,319. These figures are singularly close to the corresponding figures for the central Government.

We will consider briefly the finances of Local Government with regard chiefly to their bearing upon the general finance of the country.

The receipts are, in round numbers of millions, 82 from rates, 27 from Government, 50 from municipal enterprises or "undertakings," 24 from loans, and 17 from miscellaneous sources. The receipts from rates are only 41 per cent. of the total of 200 millions, but we must bear in mind that expenditure includes a large amount in respect of undertakings, and that against receipts from loans we have expenditure to pay off interest and capital on existing loans. It is in the main upon rates and upon Exchequer contributions that the local authorities have to rely.

Among other duties, the local authorities must keep in order the roads and pavements, light the streets, provide the sewers, pay for the police, and render other services which add to the value of the property assessed. In so far as this is the case the rates are, in the language of Mr. Goschen, an investment. Such services are sometimes called *beneficial*, as distinct from *onerous*, but the distinction has little to commend it. Just as the expenditure on the Navy, though onerous, is undoubtedly beneficial, so the poor rate and the education rate are of benefit to the whole country, and nothing is gained by thinking of them as onerous. Having regard to the services rendered by local authorities, and to the number and wealth of the population, we may brush aside any suggestion that the rates are a burden of crushing magnitude. The question how far our rating system is fair as between different localities and between different classes of the community is one of some difficulty. Two Reports have in recent years been presented to Parliament on the subject—by a Royal Commission in 1901 and by a Departmental Committee in 1914. The War has overshadowed the problem for the last five years, but it is likely to become acute in the near future.

The Government contributions are to some extent a payment for services rendered. The Crown is not liable to pay rates, and Government property is not assessed by the local authorities. But it would be manifestly unfair that the residents in a particular district should provide at their expense the cost of services rendered locally to Government in respect of streets, sewers, water, etc., and Government therefore contributes, as an act of grace, a payment in lieu of rates, based upon an assessment made by a Government official. Attempts have been made to distinguish between the national services of local authorities and their other services. It is argued, for example, that education and poverty are matters of national concern. If every area were left to deal unaided with its own children, poor, police, main roads, and other matters, the poorer areas would be charged much more heavily than the wealthy ones, which would have higher rateable values and lower expenses. The fact that an overburdened central Government hands over some of its functions to Local Government, which is often in a position to discharge them more economically and efficiently, is no reason why the taxpayer at large should be relieved at the expense of the less fortunate groups of ratepayers. Government therefore makes an annual contribution from the public purse towards the needs of local authorities.

It may be worth while to notice that in considering the total cost of our Government, national and local, we must make allowance for this contribution, amounting in 1913 to £27 m. Thus, if we take the cost of Government at £197 m. and of Local Government at £200 m., we must not assume a total of £397, but only of

£370, as the £27 m. figures twice over—once in the expenditure of Government as paid out of the Exchequer to local authorities, and again in the expenditure of these authorities.

The financial relations between the central and the local Government are complicated. If we go back to 1888, we find that Parliament made every year grants to local authorities in aid of police, poor relief (including the care of pauper lunatics), main roads, sanitary officers, and elementary education. Under the Local Government Act, 1888, the Exchequer grants for all these services except elementary education were discontinued, and in their place the produce of certain taxes was assigned to the County Councils and County Borough Councils created under that Act. In 1890 the Local Taxation (Customs and Excise) Act allotted the English share of certain duties on beer and spirits as to a fixed sum of £300,000 in aid of Police Pension Funds, and as to the residue to the County Councils and County Borough Councils in aid of rates, with an option to apply it to technical education.

In 1896 the Agricultural Rates Act relieved occupiers of agricultural land from one-half of their poor rates and borough rates, the deficiency to be made good from the Exchequer on the basis of one-half the rates then paid on such land.

The Education Acts of 1902 and 1903 absorbed the voluntary schools into the national system, and put the financial responsibility for their maintenance on the local Education Authorities. An Exchequer grant was made of 4s. for each child, and an additional 1½d. for every complete 2d. per scholar by which the produce of a penny rate falls short of 10s. per scholar in average attendance.

The Finance Act, 1907, provided that the assigned revenues should be paid into the Exchequer instead of into the special fund of the Local Taxation Account, the Exchequer being charged with the payments of the annual produce year by year. In 1908 the power to levy certain licences was transferred to the councils. The licences are issued at the Post Offices, and a grant of £40,000 is made to the councils for expenses of collection. In 1910 and 1911 Acts were passed to fix the amounts annually payable to local authorities in respect of carriage and motor-car licences, liquor licences, and local taxation (Customs and Excise) duties, at amounts equal to those produced in the year 1908–09.

The Old Age Pensions Act of 1908 considerably eased the cost of the burden of poor relief to local authorities.

The Development and Road Improvements

Act, 1909, set up a new authority, the Road Board, with power to make and improve roads. The help thus given to local authorities has been to some extent neutralised by the fixing of the amount received for carriage and motor-car licences at the 1908-09 level.

Finally, the National Health and Unemployment Insurance Act, 1911, and the provision made for sanatoria and for combating tuberculosis tend further to diminish the charges upon local authorities for providing for the sick and poor.

The general tendency of local expenditure to growth is so marked that the cost of what are called the "national" services—Poor Relief, Lunatics, Police, Main Roads, and Sanitary Officers—has trebled in twenty years. The main causes of this increase are growth of population (especially urban), extended legislation imposing new duties or giving new powers (such as for housing of the working classes), and the progress of medical, sanitary and engineering practice, leading to more elaborate and costly methods of sewerage, sewage disposal, hospital treatment, etc.

All this development of Local Government, the creation of new duties, the increased expense of carrying out those duties, partly because of better and more costly methods and partly because of the growth of the community, have

made it a difficult matter for Local Government
authorities to meet their expenses out of rates.
The principal complaints of the ratepayer are—
(a) That the State does not contribute enough
towards the cost of " national " services; (b) that
the burden of these services is unequal as between
districts; (c) that there is a want of variety in the
means of raising local revenues; (d) that those
who possess property which is not rateable occupy
an unduly favourable position; and (e) that the
burden is unduly heavy upon persons engaged in
agriculture and other occupations who require
an amount of rateable property large in proportion to their ability to pay. If we take two
shopkeepers, side by side, one of them dealing
in bulky objects like furniture, which take up
a lot of space and require large premises, and
another dealing, say, in jewellery, which requires
little space in proportion to its value, they may
be making equal profits, while the first is burdened
with much heavier rates than the second. There
is also a grievance connected with the rating of
machinery fixed to the soil, which is classed as
real and not as personal property. The question
of incidence, of course, arises—whether the shop-
keeper or manufacturer passes on the rate-
charge to his customers in the price of his goods
or whether he has to bear part or all of the

special expense himself. Such questions are among the most difficult with which the economist is confronted, owing to the uncertainty as to the facts and the weight to be assigned to them in particular cases.

The question whether, and if so when, local authorities ought to undertake business or trading enterprises has been a subject of much controversy. A large factor in its development has been the liability of local authorities to keep the roads in repair. When the streets of a city are liable to be taken up for the construction or repair of sewers, watermains, gaspipes, electric light and power cables, telegraphs and telephone wires, tramway lines, etc., and when a number of separate companies take up the roads one after another, the local residents find the use of the roads denied to them at frequent intervals. By having all these businesses in their own hand the local authorities are able to open up the roads and to overhaul the services which make use of them at one and the same time. The profits made by such companies are, of course, an additional attraction to direct management. It may be said that local authorities could charge a rent or royalty upon the profits of a company to which it concedes a right to take up its roads, but if this merely results in increased charges to residents, what is gained in one way is lost in another. A claim on the part of local authorities to fix the prices would probably be objected to, and direct management is usually the only alternative to leaving the companies a free hand in this respect.

How far municipal enterprise has, so far, justified itself is not easily ascertained, owing to the difficulty of securing proper trading accounts. The receipts and expenditure should carefully distinguish between current and capital operations; proper sinking-fund allowances should be made and depreciation allowed for; the fact should not be left out of account that, whereas a private company would pay rates, the local authority does not pay rates to itself; and even then the true figure of profit and loss, if ascertained, does not necessarily prove the wisdom or unwisdom of municipal management. It is sometimes urged that it is unjustifiable for a local authority to make a profit, for example, on its tramways. Such a profit is at the expense of those who use the trams and pay more than the cost price of the service, while the profit goes to relief of rates and so benefits those who do not ride in trams. Conversely, a loss means that the ratepayers who do not use the trams are being made to pay in order to enable other persons to ride at less than cost price. If the service is one of such general utility as the provision of water, the objection is not so strong, as a high or low charge for the service is offset to some extent by a reduced or increased rate. Amateur management or mismanagement, bungling direction, political corruption in the form of jobbing friends into posts for which they are not competent, are, where they exist, sources of additional expense to the ratepayer; but he has the remedy in his hands, and can turn out delegates who abuse their trust or show themselves bad men of business. We may say with confidence that the best directions for municipal enterprise are undertakings of public utility likely to be better conducted collectively in the public interest than by private enterprise, which looks primarily to profit. It is implied in this condition that the business to be managed should be tolerably simple and straightforward.

Assuming, then, that municipal enterprise is reasonably well conducted and that its charges are fair, we may conclude that its cost is no real burden upon the ratepayers, who are merely buying necessary services at a proper price. They are only penalised in so far as the charges are higher or the service worse than if the business were in private hands.

Receipts from Loans, £24 m., may be briefly dismissed. Loans are controlled by Government in such a way as to assure that they are justified in their object, and that arrangements are made, not only for paying the interest, but for wiping off the principal by annual instalments. If a new cemetery is needed, it would be very disturbing to require the whole cost to be met from the rates of one year, and the resort to a loan enables the cost to be spread over a period not longer than the cemetery is likely to prove sufficient. The general position as to local loans will be considered later.

The Miscellaneous Revenue, £17 m., includes nearly £6 m. from rents, interest, sales of property, etc. Over £2 m. were received for fees, fines, penalties, and licences, and about £1⅓ m. for repayments on account of private improvements executed by local authorities.

Turning to the expenditure side, we have the following table:

EXPENDITURE BY LOCAL AUTHORITIES, 1913.
(ooo's omitted).

	£
Town and municipal authorities for police, sanitary and other public works, etc.	127,987
Unions and parishes for poor relief, etc.	20,673
County authorities for police, lunatic asylums, etc.	27,531
Rural District and Parish Councils, etc.	6,185
School Boards and Secondary Education Committees (Scotland)	4,562
Harbour authorities	11,558
Other authorities	1,582
	200,080

It is to be noted that Irish police and education are mainly provided from Imperial funds not included in these figures.

The outstanding debts of local authorities on the 31st of March, 1914, were about £655 m. Against this may be set properties which have been valued roughly at £1,500 m. The figure is, of course, highly conjectural. Mr. Pethick Lawrence pertinently says: " What is the value of a main road a hundred miles long ? Its actual area valued as agricultural land may be worth some £30,000, but the community has probably spent many times this amount in bringing it to its present condition, and would lose untold wealth if it were done away with." Similar remarks apply to bridges, sewers, etc. Many of the properties of local authorities are productive of revenue, and others have a considerable selling value. A list of such properties would include lands, parks, gardens, cemeteries, municipal buildings, such as schools, workhouses, asylums, markets, baths, piers, docks, harbours, quays, canals, and the assets of going concerns, like waterworks, gas and electricity works, tram-ways, etc. In view of the increased population and rateable value, and the enlarged functions of Local Government, the growth and extent of local loans is by no means so alarming as is often supposed.

7

THE BUDGET OF 1919

W E have now examined the financial record of a specimen year, the last before the War, with the object of seeing how the figures of our National Finance are to be read. The War upset everything, Finance included, and the figures since 1913 are abnormal both in form and in substance. Instead of voting annually so much for the Army, the Navy, and the new Air Services, Parliament has passed huge Votes of Credit for War expenditure without a disclosure of details of the purposes for which the money was provided, and large sums have been borrowed in various forms, including the issue of Treasury notes greatly in excess of the gold reserve held for their redemption.

It will bring our information up to date and test our power of understanding our financial position if we read an abridged report of the Budget speech made by the Chancellor of the Exchequer in the House of Commons on the 30th of April, 1919.

Mr. CHAMBERLAIN, Chancellor of the Exchequer, said: People during the War accepted the immense burdens of the War without grumbling, and the House of Commons passed them with the minimum of criticism. But both the House and the people are in a different mood to-day. I am called upon at one and the same time to remit or to repeal the taxation which was imposed and to remedy all the grievances which have been cheerfully endured in these years of stress and strain, not merely to resume the civil expenditure which was interrupted under the stress of war, but to provide the means for creating within a few months or a few years a new heaven and a new earth. The same people who call upon me for fresh and large expenditure in every special field expect me at the same time to accomplish vast reductions in expenditure. I can work no such marvel, and unless I can have not merely the good will, but the assistance of Parliament, the task which confronts me is one which no man can complete.

The expenditure—the Exchequer issues for the year which has just been completed—was less than the estimate of £2,972,000,000 by £393,000,000. The estimate of daily average expenditure was £8,143,000, and the actual expenditure was £7,067,000. In the earlier period, from the 1st of April to the 9th of November, it was £7,443,000; in the later period, from the 10th of November to the 31st of March, it was £6,476,000. That is a reduction of £1,667,000 per day on the Budget Estimate, or, in other words, a reduction of 20 per cent. That reduction would have been still greater but for special expenditure consequent on and the result of demobilisation. For instance, £52,000,000 was spent on gratuities to members of the forces who were demobilised, and unemployment—a charge arising out of demobilisation—has cost £13,000,000. There has been a saving on the year in the debt charge, compared with the estimate, of £45,000,000.

If I turn from the expenditure side of the account to the revenue side, the estimate was for £842,000,000 in round numbers. The actual receipts were £889,000,000; in other words, the receipts exceeded the estimate by £47,000,000. There is an increase under Inland Revenue on every important head of duty except three. Income-tax and supertax realised just about £750,000 more than the estimate—a very remarkable approximation, I think, on a total of £291,000,000. The Death Duties failed to reach the estimate by £1,200,000, but that was one of those accidents to which we shall always be subject as long as a considerable portion of the Death Duties is derived from very large estates, because those large estates are not sufficient in number to give us a stable annual average. Had the year closed a week later the payment of duties on two estates would have brought up the receipts to the amount of the Estimate. Excess Profits Duty showed a larger deficiency below the estimate. It was down £15,000,000, but that indicates no loss of revenue except for the year. What was not paid last year will be paid this year.

Stamps are an uncertain revenue apt to disappoint the Chancellor of the Exchequer.

In the year which has closed they have done remarkably well. Even apart from the new cheque duty they have beaten all previous records. The total yield was nearly £12,500,000, representing an excess of more than £3,000,000 over the estimate and of £4,000,000 over the receipts for the preceding year. The produce of the increased cheque duty has been more than double the estimate of £750,000, a result which is due in part to the bankers having sent in for embossment with additional stamps larger stocks than were anticipated, and in part to the fact that the imposition of the tax would seem hardly to have restricted the use of cheques at all. The duties on conveyances yielded nearly £1,000,000 more than in the preceding year, due to the large number of sales of property that have taken place. Transfers on stocks and shares account for a further £400,000 of the increase, and the yield of the Companies Capital Duty has risen by over £500,000.

Customs and Excise have also done well. They show a surplus over the estimate of £14,520,000. Tobacco was up £5,750,000, spirits were up £3,000,000, tea showed an excess over the estimate of over £2,000,000, and the entertainment tax contributed £1,500,000. Only beer showed a small deficit compared with the estimate. Of the other items on the revenue side I need only mention the Miscellaneous Revenue, which contributes £37,000,000 out of a total excess of £47,000,000.

The excess was composed as to £33,000,000 of a contribution from India, on account of the £100,000,000 of Five per Cent. War Loan for which she undertook to be responsible. A further sum of £2,500,000 represents additional grants from the Colonies, making £4,500,000 in all; £1,500,000 was due to extra profits of the Mint, chiefly arising from the large demand for silver coinage.

If we now compare the two sides of the account, we find that the Exchequer issues were £2,579,301,000. The revenue was £889,021,000, leaving a deficiency to be made good by borrowing of £1,690,280,000 cash, or nearly £440,000,000 less than was anticipated a year ago. Of the total expenditure in 1918–19, 34·47 per cent. was provided by revenue, while 65·53 per cent. was provided by borrowing. If we take the figures for the five years from the 1st of April, 1914, to the 31st of March, 1919, the proportions are 28·49 per cent. from revenue and 71·51 per cent. by borrowing. That is a record which I believe no other belligerent can equal, and the sacrifices which it indicates place us in a good position to face our future difficulties. The borrowing to meet the deficiency on the year of £1,690,280,000 has been under the following main heads:—National War Bonds, £986,000,000; War Savings Certificates, £89,000,000; and Other Debt, £400,000,000, of which £325,000,000 was advanced by the American Government and the rest derived from various other loans abroad. The balance has been provided mainly by the Floating Debt. These figures are given net and represent the face value, excluding premiums, of the securities issued except in the case of War Savings Certificates, the figure for which is taken at the cash receipt of 15s. 6d. per certificate.

This brings me to the amount of the National Debt. The National Debt proper, exclusive of what we call " Other Capital Liabilities," was, at the outbreak of the War, approximately 645 millions. On the 31st of March last year the total was, in round figures, 5,872 millions. On the 31st of March this year the total was 7,435 millions, as against the estimate a year ago of 7,980 millions. Of the capital debt incurred, interternal debt accounts for, approximately, 6,085 millions, and the external debt, approximately, 1,350 millions. A large part of the debt is represented by National War Bonds repayable at a premium. The premiums of these bonds represent a further liability of £51,716,000. Further, the War Savings Certificates are allowed for at 15s. 6d. If they were all held for five years they would be repayable at £1, and would then involve an additional obligation of 65 millions.

Finally, our foreign debt is largely repayable in foreign currency, and the sterling equivalent of the debt must necessarily vary according to the state of the exchanges at the time when repayment becomes due. Against this large total we hold certain assets. First, there are the obligations of our Allies and Dominions, amounting on the 31st of March of this year to £1,739 millions. Of that sum £171 millions were due by the Dominions and £1,568 millions by the Allies. Russia owes £568,103,000, France £434,490,000, Italy £412,520,000, Belgium £86,779,000, Serbia £18,643,000, and other Allies £47,915,000. Next to this debt from the Dominions and Allies there is the remaining liability of India in respect of the Five per Cent. War Loan, which amounts to about £30,000,000. There are also assets of a substantial character acquired out of Votes of Credit and now no longer required, and which will be disposed of as opportunity offers. Finally, there are the payments that we shall receive in respect of indemnity from our enemies. But when every proper allowance is made for these assets—the amount and value of which as well as the date at which we may expect to receive payment for them is necessarily uncertain— the burden of debt left to us is still very formidable.

The increase in the estimates of expenditure, as compared with last year, is apparent only, and due to the provision in the Votes for charges which have hitherto been borne in Votes of Credit. Moreover, a very large part of these Estimates, approximately £275,000,000 out of a total sum of £495,000,000, is due to expenditure on temporary charges arising out of the War.

Since the Estimates were published it has been necessary to assume new obligations and loans to our Allies to the amount of £28,000,000. There are liabilities of £20,000,000, as explained by my honorable friend, the Parliamentary Secretary to the Board of Trade to-day in respect of coal. Further, unemployment benefit has been extended for a further period, though at reduced rates, and I have to provide £8,000,000 additional for that purpose. Then I have to provide out of the Consolidated Fund capital for loan expenditure under the Land Settlement Bill, and I estimate it for the current year at £5,000,000. Finally, there is an additional Civil Service war

bonus under the recent award of the Arbitration
Board, which may cost us another £4,000,000
in the course of the year. I must therefore allow
in my calculation for an excess of at least
£65,000,000 on the Estimates as at present
presented. The only other item of expenditure
with which I need deal is the Debt Charge. I put
this at £360,000,000, of which £29,800,000 will
be required for service within the fixed Debt
Charge, and the balance, £330,200,000, for
services outside that charge, including the new
borrowing to be effected during the year. Under
the present circumstances, so long as borrowing
must continue, I cannot make provision for a
sinking fund. The total expenditure for the
current year, after allowing for the additional expenditure which I have just described, will be
£1,434,910,000.

What revenue have we got to set against that ?
On the existing basis of taxation we expect to
collect during the coming year a revenue of
£1,159,650,000, an increase, without any alteration in revenue, of £270,629,000 over the actual
receipts of last year. It includes a sum of
£300,000,000 on account of excess profits duty
and of £210,000,000 for miscellaneous revenue,
of which £200,000,000 are receipts from the
realisation of Vote of Credit assets. The sum
taken on account of excess profits duty may be
counted upon whatever be the decision of the
House in respect of that duty. It represents
tax due to accounting periods already closed, or,
indeed, running out, and even if the tax were
brought to an end as rapidly as possible there
would remain to be paid £300,000,000 in the

current year, and I anticipate £100,000,000 in the year after.

As regards the £200,000,000 which I have taken as the probable receipts from Vote of Credit assets this year, this figure, of course, does not represent the total amount of these assets, nor even the total amount expected to be realised in the present year. It is the amount of cash which we hope will be paid into the Exchequer over and above the very considerable amounts from the same source which are appropriated in aid of Votes. I give the figures: In aid of the Ministry of Munitions, £140,000,000; in aid of the Ministry of Shipping, £50,000,000; at the War Office, £50,000,000; at the Admiralty, £14,000,000—together, £254,000,000; making, with the £200,000,000 which I expect to receive into the Exchequer, a total for the year of £454,000,000. That does not exhaust the amount of the credit which we expect to realise. I put the total value of the assets outstanding on the 31st of March last at approximately £800,000,000. There will therefore be a further sum to come in in future years. The £200,000,000 estimated for this year is a provisional figure.

Resuming what I have said, the position for 1919–20 would then be as follows: An expenditure of £1,434,910,000, a revenue of £1,159,650,000, and a deficit, therefore, on balance of £275,260,000 —a lesser deficit, I think, than most people have anticipated. We are left, therefore, with a deficit of £275,000,000 for the current year, or, as I would prefer to call it, £300,000,000, in order to allow for contingencies and further demands, some of which I can already see maturing. That, therefore, is, I hope, the maximum figure of new money which on balance we shall need to have borrowed at the end of the year. It may be reduced by any sums which we receive, if we receive such in the course of the year, on account of repayment of capital, or payment of interest on their loans by our Allies, or in the shape of indemnities from the enemy countries, and, of course, it would be reduced to the extent of any increase of new taxation in the current year.

That is not an unreasonable figure, but I beg the Committee not to think for a moment that it is any measure of the effort that is required. In the first place, the early months of the year are from the revenue point of view always lean, and we have to borrow in anticipation of the revenue coming in. In the second place, a large part of our debt—no less than £957,000,000—is in the form of Treasury bills, and for the most part of three-monthly bills, which therefore fall due for repayment every quarter. In other words, we have to borrow that sum of money four times over in the course of the year. During the War these bills were largely used by the public as a means for the temporary investment of funds intended on the cessation of the War to be employed in industry and commerce; and as they are withdrawn for that purpose, the difficulty of borrowing to replace them would be no less great than the difficulty of new borrowing. It will, in fact, be new borrowing.

We have, in addition, the maturing in the current year of Ways and Means Advances of £455,000,000; Exchequer bonds of £245,000,000, including the figure, £66,000,000 of 1922 bonds, which have an option of redemption on the 1st of October) and the foreign debt of £96,000,000—together, £796,000,000; making, with the Treasury bills, a total of £1,753,000,000. The floating debt on the 31st of March this year amounted in round figures to £1,412,000,000—namely, £957,000,000 of Treasury bills and £455,000,000 for Ways and Means Advances, an increase in the year 1918–19 of £223,584,000.

This sum is less than the amount outstanding at the half-year ended the 30th of September, 1918, and much less than the maximum of £1,550,000,000 which was reached on the 31st of December, 1918. The drop is, of course, in part due to the collection of revenue, but it is mainly owing to the large subscriptions in War Bonds in January last as a result of the special effort and special campaign then taken in hand, which brought the floating debt down to £1,380,000,000.

Another question closely connected with the floating debt is the continued expansion of the currency note issue. (Cheers.) On the 1st of April, 1918, the amount of notes outstanding was £228,000,000. This figure had increased by the date of the Armistice to £291,000,000. On the 31st of March of this year it stood at £328,000,000, and on the 23rd of April it had risen to £349,000,000. The gold reserve remains stationary at £28,500,000, the balance being covered by Government securities. The Bank of England note issue has increased since 1st April, 1918, by £23,000,000. The aggregate amount of legal tender money in the country, which is estimated to have amounted at the beginning of the War to about £214,000,000, is now more than

£540,000,000. It is obvious that that expansion cannot be allowed to continue indefinitely. (Cheers.) But the remedy is not so simple as at first sight it seems. It is to be remembered that there has never at any period during the War or since been anything in the nature of a forced issue. Currency notes have only been issued in response to the public demand for currency. If there was anything like a forced issue it could be stopped to-day not only without disadvantage, but with positive advantage to all concerned. What would be the effect of such action under present circumstances ? The refusal of the Treasury to issue any more currency notes would not lessen the demand of the manufacturer on his banker for legal tender, and the banker would be forced to meet that demand so long as his customer had a balance to his credit. After exhausting his own stock of notes, he would go to the Bank of England. The Bank of England, unable to obtain currency notes, would have to meet the demand by the issue of their own notes or of sovereigns withdrawn from the reserve in the Banking Department. In order to protect that reserve from immediate exhaustion a violent rise in money rates and drastic curtailment of credit would have to take place.

This would not only have a most serious effect on the prices of securities, on wages, and on the rates charged on Government borrowing, but also on the revival of trade and industry, at a critical moment when the revival of trade and industry is the most important object we have in hand. It is to be remembered, further, that the inflation of the currency is not a peculiarity of our system; it is not confined even to the belligerent countries. It is a phenomenon of world-wide extent. A new level of world prices has got to establish itself before we can say with anything like exactness what amount of currency is required. To act before we have got that and before that level is established might easily produce evil consequences by restriction beyond what is necessary without any compensating advantage.

Lord Cunliffe's Committee went carefully into this question. They recognise clearly that the restriction of inflation is impracticable until the conclusion of the period of demobilisation and the cessation of War borrowing. Whilst a direct limitation of further currency issue is not, in my opinion, a step which is at the moment practicable, there is every reason why we should attack the underlying causes as quickly as possible. The first remedial measure is to reduce expenditure. (Cheers.) The second is to meet that expenditure as early and as fully as we can out of revenue. (Cheers.) The third is, when we are obliged to borrow, to borrow from real investors. The fourth is to repay Ways and Means advances. The fifth, and last, is to refund the immense volume of short-dated Treasury bills.

Measures like this can be rendered practicable only by the strictest national and individual economy. (Cheers.) I should like the Committee to consider for the moment what is the position. The hard, inexorable, economic facts are obscured by a fictitious appearance of wealth. (Cheers.) There is between two and three times as much legal tender money in circulation as there was before the War. The deposits of the joint-stock banks have more than doubled. The position of those banks, judged by every approved criterion of sound banking, is stronger than ever it was before. Almost the whole of their additional deposits are covered by the best of all banking assets, short-dated British Government securities. These securities, standing behind the deposits and standing behind the legal currency, represent to a large extent, not existing wealth, but wealth consumed in the operations of war which it must be our business to replace out of the exertions of the present. Both are drafts on future labour and the future creation of wealth. Pending payment there is an immense reservoir of artificial purchasing power, out of relation to the actual wealth on which it operates, and therefore diminishing in effect with each new step in its increase. Look beyond the accounts for the year and you see a different picture. We have sold a thousand millions of our foreign investments, losing an equivalent power to draw on the wealth created in foreign countries. We have incurred debt to the extent of £1,300,000,000. Against this we have claims on our Allies and on our Dominions; but the position of our debtors forbids us to count on these claims for much large immediate relief. Ultimately and gradually that relief will, we hope, mature, but we cannot count upon it for immediate purposes.

For years to come a considerable part of our production must be devoted to paying our foreign creditors, and a large part to making good the

wastage and arrears of war; our roads, our
railways, and in a lesser degree, but in some
degree, our machinery suffered from the absence
during these past years of the ordinary upkeep
and development. Houses, which were in short
supply before the War, are now hopelessly in
arrear. A large part of the production of the
next year—I do not know whether I ought
not to say the next few years, but a large part
of the production of the coming year both of the
produce of labour and of capital—will be needed
to make good these losses and to pay the new
liabilities we have incurred. I beg the Committee,
therefore, to be under no misapprehension as to
the magnitude of the task which lies before us. I
repeat that there is urgent need for national and
individual economy. Nothing but a united effort
of all classes, comparable to that we have seen
in the years of war, can enable us to face the years
of difficulty which must follow on the conclusion
of so great a struggle.

Sir J. WALTON.—Government economy.

Mr. CHAMBERLAIN.—Government economy first
and foremost. (Hear, hear.)

That review of our position brings me to the
consideration of the policy which we ought to
follow. The deficit of the current year on the
present basis of taxation is, as I have said,
£275,000,000, or £300,000,000. The current
year is a wholly abnormal year. Expenditure
is swollen by the overlapping of war charges.
Peace is not yet signed, and even when peace
is signed war charges continue. On the other
hand, the revenue receipts are swollen by sums
arising out of the conclusion of the War, and the

result is that neither side of the balance-sheet gives us a complete, true picture of our normal post-War position. But if this year is abnormal next year, if not equally abnormal, will at least be similarly disturbed alike by the overlap of war charges and the overlap of war receipts. The expenditure side will be swollen by demands arising out of demobilisation, out of the condition of the railways, and out of the coal production. On the other hand, there will be an overlap of existing excess profits duty and an overlap of receipts from the sale of vote of credit assets. Neither this year, nor next year, nor perhaps the year after, will therefore be entirely normal, and in inviting the Committee to consider what our policy ought to be, I am driven to the hazardous expedient of casting my mind forward into the future to an imaginary normal year.

The Committee will recognise at once what a dangerous and difficult experiment that is to make. I recall but one case in which it was attempted. Mr. Gladstone in 1853 forecast an expenditure over a period of seven years, and almost before his speech was uttered his calculations were upset by the outbreak of the Crimean War. God forbid that my calculations, after all we have gone through, should be upset by a similar cause, but apart from that I cannot conceal from myself that I may be wrong in all assumptions I make, and that I must be wrong in many. But I must have some basis on which to ask the Committee to proceed, and, as far as such a thing is possible, the future should be laid open so that members may see something of what is in prospect. For reasons which I will explain later, I shall assume that by that time the excess profits duty as we now know it will have ceased to exist. I assume it will come to an end by the time of this normal year. I shall assume, further, that the available assets out of votes of credit have all been realised and that no further funds will be drawn from them. I shall leave out of account for the present the sums we may expect to receive on account of indemnities from the enemy and in payment of interest and repayment of capital lent to our Allies. I shall present a picture of our liabilities and our resources standing by themselves alone. I think that will be the best picture, and the necessary reductions can be made later when knowledge is more exact.

On this basis I estimate the revenue of the future normal years on the existing basis of taxation at £652,000,000, made up of £198,000,000 derived from Customs and Excise, £400,000,000 from Inland Revenue, and £54,000,000 from other sources. The calculation of our expenditure in that imaginary year is an even more difficult and hazardous task. I can only tell the Committee the hypothesis on which it seems to me most nearly to approximate to the probable truth. For the purpose of my balance-sheet I assume that the deficit on the railways and the coal mines is made good, and I know nothing more urgent than that steps should be taken to deal with both of these deficits. I assume that all fresh loans to the Allies will cease, and that other abnormal expenditure, notably that in connection with the Ministries of Labour, Food, and Shipping, will also have terminated.

Then comes a more uncertain item. What am I to estimate for the Army and Navy ? what am I to put down for the new Air Force ? For the purposes of my balance-sheet I have assumed the figure for the three forces at £110,000,000, being rather more than a 40 per cent. increase on the cost of the Army and Navy before the War. We all hope that as a result of the Peace Conference the demilitarisation of Europe may be effected without fresh naval competition being started in any other quarter. I hope that it may be possible, and I believe it should be possible, to reduce the numbers both of the Army and the Navy; but whatever reduction may be possible, in that respect the pay will be higher, material will be more expensive, and none of these factors, numbers, pay, or cost of material, are yet capable of exact estimation. I give my figure for what it is worth. You can vary my calculations according to your own estimates of whether I have placed them too high or too low. The debt charge I place at £400,000,000, including a sinking fund of ½ per cent. The Civil Services at £190,000,000; Customs, Inland Revenue, and Post Office at £53,000,000; and other services at £13,000,000; making a total expenditure of £766,000,000, against which, as I have told the Committee, I can count only on a revenue of £652,000,000, leaving a deficit of £114,000,000. I propose to ask the Committee to raise this amount approximately, not all in the current year, but by taxes which in the full year would bring in approximately that figure. On the assumption that my calculations are not unduly sanguine, on the assumption, further, that they

are not upset by forces beyond our own control,
and on the yet further assumption, about which
I feel as much hesitation as anyone, that Parliament will husband our resources and observe
economy, the Committee knows the work which
it has to face, and any funds received in repayment from our Allies or in indemnities from our
enemies will be available in so far as they are
capital for the reduction of our National Debt,
and in so far as they are interest charges for the
relief of our own interest charges, and either way
indirectly for the relief of the burdens which
I am now going to ask the Committee to assume.

Before explaining the methods by which he
proposed to raise this large sum, the Chancellor
dealt with two subjects, the first of which was
land values duties. He said: I do not need
to remind the Committee that at the time of their
birth those duties were the subject of fierce and
prolonged debate (hear, hear), and as fate would
have it the Prime Minister and I took opposite
sides. There is a certain delicacy in a Chancellor
of the Exchequer touching the handiwork of
his existing chief, and it is not made easier if the
Chancellor of the Exchequer before being a
Minister serving under the Prime Minister was
one of his most active opponents (hear, hear);
but fortunately on this occasion I have the benefit
of the advice of the Prime Minister instead of
having to fear his opposition. (Cheers.) And
I am glad to be relieved of that by at once stating
that the Prime Minister and myself, no less than
the rest of our colleagues in the Government,
are entirely agreed as to the course that ought
to be pursued. (Hear, hear.) Hon. members

interested in this subject know that from the first the Revenue yield of these duties has been disappointing, but that is not all, and it is not the worst. For one reason and another, in consequence in part perhaps of the original character of the taxes, in part of the inherent difficulties of attempting at one and the same moment to carry out all over the country a new and unparalleled valuation and simultaneously to raise revenue upon it, and in part, and in no small part, owing to decisions of the Courts, the legal propriety of which I must not be thought for a moment to question, the tax by now has become unworkable. (Cheers.) In certain cases duty is declared to be leviable in circumstances in which Parliament never intended to exact it, and in which admittedly it would be unfair and contrary to the public interest to levy it, and legislation to reverse that judgment was only held up in consequence of the outbreak of war. In other cases the taxes, owing to other decisions, cannot be levied, nor can even a valuation be made upon which any tax can be levied. The result is, as I say, that the taxes in their present form are unworkable. They must either be amended or repealed. They cannot be left indefinitely as they are.

But if I were to attempt the task of amendment or repeal at this moment in the present divided state of public opinion on the subject, and in the absence of full knowledge as to the facts of the case, I should be inviting, as we hope on the eve of the conclusion of peace, a recrudescence of all the old controversies which we have forgotten during the War. Under the circumstances

the Prime Minister and I joined in recommending to the Cabinet that before action is taken the
present position of the duties should be referred
to a Select Committee of this House in order
that they may explore it, and may recommend
a course of action in regard to it. We hope that
such a careful inquiry, before which all parties
can be heard, may secure something in the nature
of common agreement as to the best course to
pursue in future.

It is fair that I should add that whilst neither
the Prime Minister nor I wish to prejudge or
to attempt to prejudice the decision which
such a Committee may form upon the duties or
upon any taxation which may be introduced in
their place, we both think it is of importance that
there should be a trustworthy valuation of the
land of the country available for public purposes
whenever it is required. (Cheers.)

I must say something about motor spirit.
(Hear, hear.) It was imposed by the 1909
Budget. The full duty, formerly 3d. per gallon,
raised in 1915–16 to 6d., applies only to cars used
for private purposes. Cars used for trade or
husbandry, hackney cars, cars of doctors or
veterinary surgeons when used for professional
purposes, are all entitled to a rebate of half
the duty. Motor fire-engines and certain other
cars are entitled to free spirit. Petrol used by
stationary engines, motor-boats, and aeroplanes,
or for cleaning purposes is also free. In 1913–14
the year before the War, about 47,000,000 gallons
paid full duty, over 40 millions paid half duty,
and about 8 millions were delivered free of duty.
I think the Committee will see that a tax of that

character is open to serious objection. (Hear,
hear.) It is complicated, and therefore expensive to administer and collect. (Hear, hear.)
In the second place, the test of dutiability is not in
the nature of the article, but in the use to which
it is applied. The same quality of spirit is
dutiable if applied to one purpose, and not
dutiable if applied to another.

The machinery for differentiating the duty
prescribed in the Act is that the duty is to be
collected at the full rate and repayment made
where the user is entitled to an abatement.
In practice the extreme inconvenience of this
is overcome in the case of some large users, such
as the London Omnibus Company, but the
examination of the claims for rebate from small
owners gives rise to an immense amount of
trouble and an immense consumption of time and
irritation, which is correlative not to the value of
the tax so much as to the trouble of investigating
the claim; and, lastly, as the Committee will
observe, in a tax of that kind so levied there
is a wide opportunity for evasion and for fraud.
(Hear, hear.) I think there will be a great deal
to be said for levying the charge, whatever it
may be that we wish to levy, on the users of
motor-cars in some other form than in the form
of petrol, but a satisfactory scheme of licensing
could only be worked out after conference with
the various interests affected, and I desire before
making any proposals on the subject to have the
advantage of the advice and assistance of the
Minister of Ways and Communications as soon
as the House has placed him in the saddle. I
propose, therefore, to discuss this question with

him in the interval between the present and the next Budget, and I hope by next Budget day that I or my successor may be in a position to make proposals in regard to them.

As to the existing Excise duty on motor spirit, that duty yields only a trifling revenue of some £50,000 a year, derived entirely, I think, from Scottish shale oil. But a difficult position has recently arisen in regard to benzol manufactured in this country. Before the War benzol was one of those spirits which were occasionally and experimentally used for propelling motor-cars, but were not taxed when so used. In refraining from taxing it the Board of Customs and Excise acted upon instructions issued by the present Prime Minister, and announced in the House of Commons in the early days of the new tax, to the effect that they were to aim at the taxation of spirit which was ordinarily and generally used for driving motor vehicles, and not to attempt to levy the tax on the various substances which, though not generally used as motor-car fuel, could be or were occasionally used as substitutes for or in association with it. That was the position up to the War. The War has changed the position completely. During the War the production of benzol for war purposes was stimulated by the Munitions Department with remarkable results. There is now in existence a manufacturing industry with large stocks of spirit which the Munitions Department no longer requires, and large continuous output amounting now to about 100,000 tons a year, of which 70,000 tons, or thereabouts—that is equivalent to 21 million gallons—is available for motor fuel. The Minister for Munitions promised to hand over these stocks to the trade for the use of motor petrol. The Petrol Control Committee undertook to release for motor fuel as much as could be put on the market. Then the Board of Customs and Excise felt it to be their duty to step in and to issue a warning that benzol so applied might be subject to taxation. I have to consider what is to be done. We have here a case of an industry found vital during the War, created and stimulated for war purposes, practically created at Government instigation and under Government guidance, and that industry is suddenly confronted with the loss of its market owing to the cessation of the War.

That is not all. Benzol is not only important to the nation as an additional indigenous source of supply of motor fuel, but it is a very important ingredient in the dyeing industry, an industry which, as the Committee knows, has been found so vital to our existence and to our trade that not only this but preceding Governments have done everything in their power to establish it and to promote its growth in this country. Under the circumstances, and acting on the advice of the Board of Trade, I propose to give legal authority for the exemption of benzol from taxation by repealing the Excise duty, and I am glad to think that the Scottish shale industry, an industry which it is also in the national interests to develop, will, of course, obtain the advantage of the repeal.

There is another subject in regard to motor spirit—viz., motor spirit licences. The motor spirit licence duty was imposed as a war measure to restrict the use of private motor-cars at a time of shortage. Its revenue effect was purely secondary. The necessity for restriction has now gone. The licence duty was collected by the Petrol Control Department of the Board of Trade, a Department which, I think, did its work extremely well, but which is now in process of being dissolved. I am told that if we abolish this small licence duty, with all its anomalies, we shall at the same time enable the Board of Trade to put an end to this Department, with its 300 officials. (Loud cheers.)

That brings me to a subject which I, at any rate, regard as the most important feature of the present Budget. I come to the establishment of Imperial Preference. I am not propounding, and cannot propound to-day, the general trade policy for this country. If the steps which are found to be necessary require legislative sanction, that sanction must be given in some other measure than the Finance Bill. For the present, my task is only to give effect and assent to the declaration of the Imperial War Cabinet and the Imperial War Conference two years ago, in which the representatives of the British Government concurred that, as soon as possible, preference on duties now or hereafter existing should be introduced for goods of Imperial origin.

The range of our present Customs duties is not wide, though it covers more articles than people are apt to suppose. Only three Colonial or British oversea products fall into the categories subject to duty at the present time in any large quantities—namely, tea, cocoa, and rum, but there are many other dutiable articles which appear in our Customs returns from His Majesty's possessions overseas. I need name only such articles as coffee, sugar, tobacco, and wine.

But though the beginnings may be small, the measure of what I am inviting the Committee to do is not the amount of British Imperial trade which secures preference at this moment, but the opportunities for the development of that trade which I invite the Committee to open out. There is room for vast extension. There never was a time when it was more important to the Empire as a whole or to us in particular that development should take place. From the small beginnings of to-day, I hope that many members of this House will live to see a really wide structure of inter-Imperial trade develop.

In deciding on the form which preference is to take I have had four main considerations before me. In the first place, the preference should be substantial in amount. In the next place, the rates should as far as possible be few and simple. Thirdly, where there is an existing Excise duty corresponding to the Customs duty which is affected, the Excise duty must be proportionately altered. We cannot give preference at the expense of the home producer. (Hear, hear.) Lastly, in carrying out this policy, I have to remember the interests of our Allies and, as far as practicable, to avoid increasing duties on their products for the purpose of giving preference.

As I have said, the range of our existing duties is small. It falls mainly into three classes: First, there are the new Customs duties imposed by Section 12 of the Finance Act (No. 2), 1915, which carry with them no corresponding Excise, on cinematograph films, clocks and watches, motor-cars and musical instruments. On these duties I propose to fix the preference at one-third, which is what I may call the general Empire rate in so far as a general Empire rate exists.

The next class comprises taxes on consumable commodities apart from alcohol. These are, in essence, revenue duties pure and simple. On these in many cases the duties are themselves very high in relation to the value of the article, and a preference of one-third would be both more than I could afford, and more than I think is necessary or justifiable. Before coming to any definite decision, I thought I ought to take consultation with the interests affected. I accordingly appointed a small Departmental Committee of representatives of the Colonial Office, the India Office, the Board of Trade, and the Board of Customs and Excise, and asked them to get into touch with representatives in this country of the producers, importers, and manufacturers of the articles affected, and to ascertain their views as to the probable effect of preference on the trade and industry of the United Kingdom and the British Possessions and on the rate of duty.

After considering the views of the interests affected, as gathered by that Committee, I have come to the conclusion that for preference on this class of articles I should be justified in recommending to the Committee a rate of one-sixth of the duty.

I ought to say at this stage that I propose that, in the two classes of goods with which I

have already dealt—viz., the duties on manufactured articles and the duties on consumable
commodities other than alcohol—the preference
should be given by way of reduction of the
existing duties on Colonial produce, and not by
way of surcharge on foreign produce.

My right hon. friend asked me to give some
further information as to the character of the
articles concerned. The most important is tea.
The estimated revenue from tea in the coming year
is, without the change in duty, £16,000,000. The
duty is 1s.; the preference will therefore be 2d.
In normal circumstances before the War, when
the importation of tea was unrestricted, nearly
90 per cent. of the tea was already Empire-grown.
The result, therefore, of the grant by way of
preference will practically be equivalent to the
reduction of the duty on tea, and I anticipate
that that will lead, as it always has led, to a
largely increased consumption. In the circumstances, the loss for a full year involved in that
preference may be put at £2,300,000, but will not
be more in the current year, which is not a
complete year, than probably £1,800,000.

The next article is cocoa. The estimated
revenue from cocoa is £2,400,000. About two-
thirds of our imports now come from Empire
sources. Preference at the rate of one-sixth
would be worth 7s. per cwt., meaning a loss of
revenue of about £200,000. The revenue from
coffee is small—£650,000—and a small proportion
—only about 20 per cent. of our imports at
present—comes from Empire sources. The
amount which could be grown in the Empire is
capable, I think, of almost limitless expansion.

(Hear, hear.) The preference of one-sixth, which is worth 7s. per cwt., would mean on the present proportion an immediate loss of revenue of £20,000. Chicory will, of course, follow coffee, as it always does, and the Excise duty will be proportionately reduced.

Now I come to sugar. The estimated Customs revenue from sugar is £39,000,000. Only a very small portion of the imports, 7 per cent., comes from Empire sources. The preference would be worth 4s. per cwt., and would mean a loss of revenue of about £500,000. The Excise duty on beet sugar produced in this country will, of course, be similarly reduced. It already stands at 2s. 4d. per cwt. less than the Customs duty. Dried fruits are only a small matter. I need not trouble the Committee with the figures, but the preference will be given on them also.

Coming now to tobacco, the estimated revenue on the present basis is £47,000,000. Only 2 per cent. of the imports come from Empire sources, but a very considerable expansion is possible. A preference of one-sixth, or 1s. 4d. per lb., on unmanufactured tobacco, a rate which governs the other duties, is a substantial one, and will, I hope, stimulate increased production in India and the Colonies concerned. The Excise duty on tobacco grown in the United Kingdom will again be correspondingly reduced. In the case of both tobacco and sugar it is proposed that the preference to the manufacturers should be based on the amount of the British-grown product in the import. With regard to motor spirit, the estimated Customs revenue from which is £2,200,000, only about 18 per cent. comes from Empire sources, and a preference of one-sixth, or 1d. per gallon, may mean a loss of revenue of about £60,000. I have decided for other reasons, as I have already explained, to recommend the abolition of the Excise duty.

I come now to the third class of dutiable articles, beer, wine, and spirits. There is no importation of Colonial beer. The arrangement of a preference would be complicated and difficult, and at any rate we may safely neglect it for the time. I propose to do the same, for the same reason, with table waters, matches, and playing-cards. Cards are hardly worth mentioning except that I might be attacked afterwards for concealing what I was doing or was not doing. The estimated revenue from wine on the present basis is £1,250,000. Only about 7 per cent. of the imports come from Empire sources at present. The industry, however, is one which is being developed, and is capable of being further developed both in South Africa and Australia, and both Dominions attach importance to it. At present the wine duty is levied at two rates—1s. 3d. and 3s. a gallon, according to strength. A preference of one-sixth on those small duties would, I am advised, be quite ineffective. On the other hand, in consideration of the interests of our Allies, notably of France and Portugal, and of some neutrals, we are unwilling at such a moment as the present to raise the duty on a very important article of their export. We propose, therefore, to give the preference by way of reduction, and to allow 6d. on the lower rate of 1s. 3d. and 1s. on the higher rate of 3s. There is an additional tax on wines imported in bottles of 1s. a gallon on still wine and 2s. 6d. on sparkling. I propose to allow 6d. preference on the first and 9d. on the second. Spirits constitute my most difficult problem. The State derives a very large revenue from the Excise duty on spirits manufactured in this country, and it is essential that preference shall not be given in a form which would appreciably reduce the yield. For that reason it is necessary to take spirits in a class apart, as an exception to the general rule which I have followed. To give a preference by reduction would involve a corresponding reduction in the Excise duty and a loss of revenue which I am unable to face. For the purpose of the duties, spirits are divided into five classes, four subject to Customs duty—rum, brandy, Geneva, and other sorts, and the fifth, home-made spirit, including whisky, subject to the Excise duty. Over 80 per cent. of the rum comes from Empire sources. The imports from the Empire of other spirits are at present small, and I think likely to continue so, at any rate for a long time to come, though they are capable of some development.

As regards the amount of the preference, I have come to the conclusion that anything like a rate of one-sixth with such high duties as are charged would be too high. It would amount to 5s. a gallon on the rate of duty in force, and a larger amount if this duty is increased. I propose, therefore, to fix the rate of preference at 2s. 6d. per gallon, not by a reduction in the duty on Colonial spirits, but by an increase in the duty on foreign spirits. That will give me a slight additional yield of revenue. The effect of the preference proposals as a whole on revenue will be a reduction of £2,500,000 in the current year, and something over £3,000,000 in the full year, and without allowing for any large increase in the imports of Colonial products. The great bulk will be in respect of tea.

Now as to the date on which preference will take effect. The general date I propose is 1st of September, so as to allow time for administrative machinery to be set up. But tea requires special treatment, as the great bulk of the supply comes from the Empire. To postpone the introduction of the new rate too long might lead to the withholding of stock, and the consumer going short. After consulting the distributing interest, I propose that the reduced duty should come into force on 2nd of June. If these results are small, it must be remembered that the immediate bulk of Colonial products affected is small, but the results both on the revenue and, as I hope, on the trade will be seen increasingly as the years go on.

At last I come to the new taxation which I propose to impose. I confine myself at this moment to saying that I do not propose to proceed with the luxury tax. I am quite ready to give my reasons for this, but I think that I should unduly delay the Committee if I did so. Dealing first with spirits, I may remind the Committee that it was found necessary to restrict the delivery of spirits from bond as from the 1st of April, 1917, to a limit not exceeding 50 per cent. of the deliveries of 1916. Owing to a variety of causes, including the restriction above referred to, the increased duty on spirits, the operation of the

9

immature spirit duty, and I am afraid I must add some withholding of stocks, the supply of spirits fell short of the demand and prices rose to an extent which led the Food Controller, in consultation with my predecessor, in the spring of last year to limit them by imposing a maximum scale of prices, which were announced by Budget day, and provided for a substantial increase in the then duty.   Two changes affecting the position have since occurred.   In the first place, the scale of prices was revised in August so as to afford relief to a section of the trade which had bought their stocks at somewhat inflated prices, and had not then had an opportunity of disposing of them. The quantities allowed to be delivered from bond were increased as from the 24th of February last from 50 to 75 per cent. of the quantities delivered in 1916, bringing the authorised clearance up to 21,400,000 gallons a year.   Both of these changes have further increased the profits of the trade, and they are now in the aggregate more than my predecessor estimated, and more than, I think, is reasonable.   The Committee will not be surprised, therefore, to learn that I propose to ask that part of these profits at any rate should be diverted to the Exchequer by a further increase in spirit duty from 30s. to 50s. per proof gallon.   This increase will involve some readjustment of trade prices to prevent the burden falling unequally on different sections of the trade.   The scale, consequently, has been revised so as to distribute the additional duty as equitably as possible throughout.   The alteration will only affect the consumer in a few cases, such as the price of spirits sold to him in bottle, or in jar or cask. Owing to the great rise in the cost of bottling and the prices fixed for the bottle and the glass respectively the sale of spirits by glass has been much more remunerative than the sale by bottle, and I think that some of the difficulties complained of in the early part of the year during the epidemic of influenza in reference to the obtaining of spirits were due to this cause. That increase will produce an additional revenue of £21,650,000 in the full year on the present authorised amount of clearance. For the current financial year, a month of which has already passed, it will bring in an increased yield of £19,850,000.

I pass by a not unnatural transition from spirits to beer. A year ago, when the authorised annual output of beer was 33⅓ per cent. of the 1916 output my predecessor found that excessive profits were being made, that the prices charged to the consumer were higher than could be justified by the then existing conditions. He accordingly decided, in consultation with the Food Controller, to increase the duty from 25s. to 50s. a barrel. At the same time the partial control of prices previously instituted was continued in a modified form. The order limiting prices did not touch sales on any portion of licensed premises other than public bars, and it did not refer to all articles sold. It did not touch draught beer above 1034 degrees or any bottled beer. The controlled prices which were fixed so as to enable the trade to secure sufficient profit without unduly raising the prices of the beer were not affected by the order. It was, however, subsequently found that for beers of higher gravity and bottled beers the prices charged were in many cases increased much beyond the limit which would have provided a reasonable profit. Further, after the armistice it became possible to some extent to meet the public demand for more and better beer, and as from the 1st of January an additional quantity has been allowed to be brewed at a higher average gravity. The increase, which was in the proportion of 25 per cent. of the standard barrelage for 1918, had, of course, the effect of reducing the cost of production, and the trade was thus in a position to make still larger profits than before. In view of that, the Government thought it right to warn the trade, that while they might have the run of those profits until Budget day, they must expect an increase of duty at that time. A new scale of prices was issued at the same time that the increased barrelage was allowed. This scale allowed a fair margin of profit for further taxation to be taken in respect of the increased barrelage.

The necessity which existed during the War of rigidly restriticng the amount of grain to be used in brewing has now passed away, and the Government, after full consideration, are prepared to take a further step in allowing increased supplies of beer and of beer of a better quality. Brewers will be accordingly allowed to increase their output by 50 per cent. on their 1918 barrelage. This, added to the 25 per cent. increase sanctioned last January, will mean that the restricted barrelage which was allowed in 1918 will be increased by 75 per cent., bringing the total authorised barrelage for the year up to 20,000,000 barrels, compared with the pre-war barrelage of 36,000,000. In order that the consumer may be able to obtain beer of better quality, brewers will be at liberty henceforth to brew to an average gravity not exceeding 1040 degrees in Great Britain, as compared with the 1032 which is the existing limit, and with the pre-war gravity of 1050 under unrestricted conditions. The average gravity of beer brewed in Ireland, which has always been higher, will remain at 1047, as compared with 1065 before the War. (An hon. member.—Why ?) In consequence of the particular conditions and character of that trade. (Laughter.) This increase in the average gravity which the brewers in Great Britain are allowed to brew will, I hope, go far to remove the grievance of which some of them have complained that they were unable to maintain their special trade at the low gravity hitherto imposed upon them. The effect of further relaxing the restrictions on output while continuing the present scale of prices to the consumer, which we do not propose to alter, will be to increase the margin of profit for taxation beyond what was contemplated when the prices were fixed in February last and the trade warned.

I now feel justified in proposing to appropriate to the Exchequer from these profits a total amount of 20s. per standard barrel by raising the duty from 50s. to 70s. In fixing this rate of duty I have had to consider the diversity of conditions existing in the trade, and to give fair consideration to those who are least fortunately situated. I will indicate very shortly the effect of the proposal on the revenue of the current year. I put my estimate of the revenue from beer on the existing basis of taxation at £37,800,000, and by the existing basis I mean the existing barrelage and the existing rate of duty before any alterations are made. Any increase of output, of course, increases the yield of the tax quite apart from any increase in duty. In estimating the additional revenue I shall secure I have to take account of both the increased number of barrels on which duty will be paid and of the increased rate of duty on each barrel so charged, and I estimate that the combined effect of these two increases will be £31,200,000 for a full year and for the current short year £22,200,000. The Government desire that I should add that the character and nature of the control to be exercised over this trade in alcoholic drink is now occupying the attention of His Majesty's Government. That is not wholly or mainly a revenue matter, but we think it right to say that should at some future time a yet further increase of barrelage be allowed, that would be a fair reason for a still further increase in taxation.

In this connection I have one small change to propose, which I think is fair and right, with the object of bringing the charges on beer made in private houses into some kind of correlation with the increased charges now made on beer brewed for sale. The provisions of the existing law are of long standing, and however appropriate they may have been to a time when the beer duty was 6s. 8d. a barrel, they are not suitable when the duty is raised to 70s. a barrel, and when brewers for sale are still restricted as regards output and gravity. I thought first of all that it might be possible, in view of the new high rates, to prohibit

domestic brewing altogether, but in deference
to an old-established custom in certain agricultural districts I refrained from taking that
course, though I could not view with equanimity
or patience a large increase of private brewing
in consequence of the increased duty imposed
upon the brewers for sale. In the case of private
brewers who now pay beer duty no change is
necessary, and they will remain as at present
liable to beer duty, subject to the nominal
registration duty of 4s. In the case of persons
who do not pay beer duty, I do not propose to
impose the beer duty, as such, but to make them
pay their contribution to the Exchequer by way
of a licence duty. The revenue effect of these
changes is negligible, except as some measure of
protection against loss of revenue from other
sources, but I think they are necessary for that
purpose and for fairness.

I turn now to direct taxation. The Excess
Profits Duty in its present form is a war tax.
It was imposed under the stress of war, and when
in the midst of the enormous burdens we had
to bear it was felt that profits in excess of pre-war
profits might justly be called upon to make
special contribution. It is open to many objections, but it was a rough-and-ready method of
justice which Parliament, in its then, happily,
not very critical mood, accepted without too
much difficulty, and the revenue results of it
have been most satisfactory during the war period.
It was imposed for the first year at 50 per cent.
then for a period at 60 per cent., and since the
1st of January, 1917, at 80 per cent. It has
been a good revenue-raiser, but there are great

objections to it. In the first place, it operates
with unfairness and inequality as between firms
with a good pre-war standard of profit and firms
with a poor pre-war standard or no pre-war
standard at all.

In the second place, at the existing high rate
it has encouraged wasteful expenditure. When
£4 out of every £5 would have gone to the State
if not spent by the owner, he was inclined to
lavish expenditure on his business. But, more
than that, it cannot be doubted that a flat rate
tax of 80 per cent. on all profits over pre-war
standards or where there was no pre-war
standard over a small margin acts as a great
deterrent to enterprise, industry, and new
development. I do not wish under these circumstances to continue the tax a moment beyond
what is necessary at so high a figure as at present.
It would be contrary to public interest, and I do
not propose to do it. On the other hand, I have
to remember that this is a war tax, that the war
expenditure is still continuing and that even after
peace is signed war expenditure and the burdens
of war will still remain, and that I am not in
a position simply to repeal the duty without
finding anything to put in its place.

Under these circumstances my first effort was
to find some form in which the profits of businesses
might be called upon to make a special contribution to the revenue of the country without
the anomalies and the objections to which the
present tax is subject. I had before me suggestions made to that effect by Sir J. Harmood-
Banner, by Mr. J. F. Mason and by Mr. Lionel
Hichens.

I had also the example of taxation imposed with similar objects both in the United States and in Canada. My information is imperfect, and the time at the disposal of myself and my colleagues has been short, and we have been subject to other daily grave preoccupations. I need not say that if a new tax is to be imposed, it would in any case be necessary that it should be carefully thought out and its advantages and disadvantages carefully weighed in order that we should not repeat the anomalies or injustices of the existing tax. Therefore the form of the tax would be of great importance, and such an inquiry takes time. I have had other suggestions made to me, but the Government have not been able to give to the subject in the weeks before the Budget the attention which it requires for a satisfactory solution. Under the circumstances, therefore, I propose to the Committee, as a temporary measure, and only as a temporary measure, to continue the existing tax for another year at the reduced rate of 40 per cent. (Cheers.) I anticipate that the yield of the excess profits duty on this basis for a full year will be £50,000,000. It must not be supposed that the yield of the 80 per cent. rate under war conditions is at all a safe guide as to the yield under post-war conditions. I have to allow for the right of recoupment which is given by statute under certain conditions to those who have paid the tax. I have to allow for the fact that the high yield of the tax, and, indeed, the initiation of the tax itself, was based upon the fact that certain businesses were making extraordinary and abnormal profits. Under these circumstances, although the estimate must, of course, be a very rough and hypothetical one, I am advised that it would not be safe to count upon a revenue of more than £100,000,000 if the tax continued at 80 per cent., and I expect a revenue of £50,000,000 at the lower rate of 40 per cent.

Now I turn to the death duties. The last alteration in the scale of the estate duty was made in the first Budget of 1914, and it has not been altered during the War. I think that my predecessors were right in so doing. Death duties are not a suitable instrument for meeting a temporary emergency. It requires a generation for all the properties subject to the tax to pass under it, and accordingly it is only when you are considering a permanent increase of revenue that the death duties ought to be raised. We have come to the time when we have to consider permanent increase of revenue, and I propose to ask the Committee to sanction such an alteration in the scale as is estimated to produce in a full year a sum of £10,000,000. No change is made in the case of estates under £15,000 in value. Estates between £15,000 and £20,000, which now pay at the rate of 5 per cent., will in future pay at the rate of 6 per cent. The present rates rise from 6 per cent. to 9 per cent. in respect of estates of between £20,000 and £100,000. A corresponding rise in the new scale would be from 7 per cent. to 14 per cent. At present an estate of £250,000 pays 12 per cent. I propose in the future that it shall pay 20 per cent. The rate is now 16 per cent. on estates of over £500,000, and the proposed new rate is 25 per cent. The maximum rate on the existing scale is 20 per cent.

applicable to estates of over £1,000,000. I propose that estates between £1,000,000 and £1,250,000 should in the future pay 30 per cent.; estates between £1,250,000 and £1,500,000, 32 per cent.; and between £1,500,000 and £2,000,000, 35 per cent.; and that estates of over £2,000,000 should pay 40 per cent., or double the existing rate. (Cheers.)

I do not attempt to hide from the Committee the fact that these are very onerous rates. They constitute, taken in conjunction with the income tax, a further differentiation between wealth derived from continuing personal exertion and wealth derived from accumulated capital, but they are more than that. They are an insurance for the safety of capital. Montesquieu said that taxation was " that part of his wealth which each citizen gave to obtain the secure enjoyment of the remainder." There has been a good deal of discussion of late about a levy or tax on capital. If by a tax on capital is meant a small annual charge, then I think that that charge is as widely distributed and more fairly and conveniently raised in the shape of our income tax. If, on the other hand, there is meant a large levy on capital, a large slice to be taken out of accumulated capital, then I beg the Committee to consider what the result might be. It is a bad time to propose such a tax when, for the past five years, you have been begging people to save, and when you are still obliged to ask them to save and to give you their savings. It is a bad time to tax those who have responded to your appeal by reducing their expenditure and making econo-mies, and to let those go free who disregarded your instructions and who spent their money when it was not in the interest of the State, or in ways which were not in the interest of the State.

Consider a levy on capital apart from the circumstances of the moment. The death duties make such a levy, and they make it once in a lifetime, at a time when the taxpayer receives an accession of income, and since they are levied only at death, and we do not all die at the same time, the process of making the valuation and of levying the tax is a task of manageable proportions. It can be done justly and fairly as between man and man, and it can be done with a minimum of evasion or of fraud. Since only a portion of the capital of the country is dealt with in any one year, the tax is paid without any disturbance of credit, and without any depreciation of securities to the detriment either of the State itself or of the home. If a levy was to be made on all the capital of the country at one and the same time by the tax collector, all these advantages would be lost. To make an efficient valuation, fair as between man and man, and fair as between the revenue and the State, would exceed the power of any revenue administration in the world, and I make bold to say that our own is the best. It would exceed their power at any time, and still more now, when the staff is still depleted owing to the War, and when they are charged with the overwhelming new responsibilities which the War has brought. It would be open to all the objections which arose and all the difficulties to which simultaneous valuation of the whole land of the country and the taxation of the land of the country gave rise under the Land Values Duty, and open to those objections on a vaster scale, because you would have to value not only real, but personal property. Since very few people would have money lying idle sufficient to pay their obligations under the tax, it would mean an immense disturbance of credit. Everyone would be seeking to sell securities of one sort or another, and where all are sellers who would be buyers, and who shall measure the loss to the country by the depreciation of all securities (cheers), and who shall measure the loss to the individual through the same cause?

If to avoid these difficulties the State takes payment in kind then all the difficulties of valuation still remain. The State cannot refuse to accept property of any kind at a valuation which itself has put upon it, and we should be left the owners of parcels of land, odd parcels of shares, in every conceivable part of the country and in every conceivable undertaking, many of them of very doubtful value and very difficult to realise. I will only add that if it were thought that this expedient, once resorted to, would, as well might be the case, and as some desire should be the case, be resorted to again at every moment of difficulty or of extravagance, it would then be the greatest possible discouragement to industry and enterprise that the mind of man or Parliament could devise. It would be the strongest deterrent to saving and the creation of new capital, and it would be the strongest incentive to wasteful expenditure and to the dissipation or withdrawal of existing capital. I say boldly that whatever be our views on the distribution of wealth or on the respective shares of the fruits of industry to which capital and management and labour are entitled, our great need now and for years to come is that we should have, not less capital, but more capital (cheers), and I hope the House will lend no countenance to so hazardous and, in my opinion, so disastrous an experiment. I estimate, as I have said, that this new scale of death duties will add £10,000,000 in a full year and £2,500,000 in this year, and it will take effect from the date of the Royal assent to this year's Finance Bill.

There is one small matter in this connection with which I must deal—the existing rate of interest charged in respect of outstanding death duties at 3 per cent. That no longer corresponds at all to the value of money. It acts as an encouragement to postpone the payment of duties. Without wishing to suggest for a moment anything in the nature of a vindictive or punitive rate, I think it would be proper now to raise the rate to 5 per cent.

Before we leave the subject of the death duties, let me say that certain relief was granted from the death duties as regards the estates of members of the Forces, mercantile marine, and fishermen. I now propose to extend these provisions in two respects. At present the death must have occurred within twelve months of the wound, accident, or disease to which it was attributable. Experience has shown that that period is not long enough to cover a considerable number of cases which fall within the spirit if not the letter of the law. I propose to extend the period to three years and to give that extension retrospective effect. (Cheers.)

Further, I hope the Committee will agree that there should be power to grant relief to persons of the categories named dying within the same period of three years as the result of wounds, accidents, or disease occurring after the War, but as a direct consequence of the War. I have in mind such cases as military operations, if they continue anywhere after peace is signed, and cases where death or accident may be due to mine-sweeping or removal of dangers which the War has left behind. Provisions to that effect will be inserted in the Finance Bill.

I come now to income tax. (Cheers.) I have already mentioned the satisfactory yield of income tax last year. In the current year we expect to do even better. Last year's income tax and super tax together produced £291,000,000. This year we estimate them to produce £354,000,000, an increase of £63,000,000, without any further change in the rates. Apart from normal growth, the increase is due to two causes—first, owing to the imposition of the tax at higher rates last year, the arrears carried forward are at a higher figure; and second, this year will see a full collection under Schedule A, whereas, owing to the introduction of the instalment system, only one-half was collected last year.

Now what am I to do about it ? The Committee knows that a Royal Commission has been appointed to investigate income tax and super tax and all the problems to which they give rise. It was recognised before the War that the time had come for such an inquiry. The higher rate has increased the anomalies of the tax and rendered greater any hardships which were endured. But the pre-War rate is nothing compared with the post-War rate. Accordingly all these anomalies and grievances pressed more urgently for consideration, and new ones were created by the circumstances of the War. I therefore appointed a Royal Commission as soon as I could after entering office. I do not know what the report of that Commission may have in store for the taxpayer or the Chancellor of the Exchequer. The taxpayer, I imagine, views it with hope. The Chancellor of the Exchequer looks forward to it with foreboding. Whatever may happen, they are likely—I think they are certain—to propose great changes, and great changes are seldom made in a tax without decreasing its yield at the then existing rate. Under the circumstances I have thought that the wisest course for me to pursue was to make no change in the income tax (cheers) pending the report of that Commission, except so far as may be necessary to carry out special undertakings already given, such, for example, as the exemption from income tax of wounds and disability pensions and of gratuities payable on demobilisation. (Cheers.) On the other hand, in pursuance of the same principle—for what is sauce for the goose is sauce for the gander—I do not propose to ask the Committee to modify this year any of the temporary reliefs from income tax or super tax which have been granted from time to time as the result of the War. I hope, whether right or wrong, that the proposals which I make with regard to the income tax are consistent proposals to be treated as a whole. I hope the Committee will treat them as such, and I think they may be encouraged by the thought that Lord Colwyn, the chairman of the Royal Commission, hopes that the Commission will be able to report in time to enable effect to be given if the House so wills to their recommendations by the Budget of next year.

I am now able to summarise the result. In a full year I should obtain, by the changes in taxation, £108,950,000, derived as to £60,000,000 from inland revenue and as to £48,950,000 from Customs and Excise, thus almost exactly meeting the deficit of £114,000,000 which I calculated we shall have to face in a future normal year. In this calculation I took no credit for the normal growth of the yield in revenue. On the other hand, I allowed very little for the normal growth of expenditure. I set one against the other. But it must be remembered that social and industrial changes now in progress, if by lessening the return on capital, they restrict the accumulation of wealth, may eat into the yield of the direct taxes, and especially of the super tax and the death duties. Again, the £50,000,000 of the £114,000,000 which is attributable to the continuation of the excess profits duty is avowedly intended only to be temporary, and must be replaced from some other source unless in the meantime we find relief from our burden in other ways. In the current year I estimate an additional revenue of £41,450,000 net.

The final balance-sheet for 1919–20 will thus be: Expenditure, £1,434,910,000; revenue, £1,201,100,000; deficit to be borrowed,

10

£233,810,000. On this basis the gross debt on the 31st of March, 1920, will be increased from £7,435,000,000 to £7,669,000,000, or, if we take the round figure of £250,000,000 as the new borrowing to allow for a margin of error, £7,685,000,000, still substantially less than the figure of £7,980,000,000 which we thought last year might be the total on the 31st of March now past. Against these future liabilities we shall hold special assets in the shape of loans to our Allies, £1,668,450,000; loans to our Dominions, £196,890,000; a further contribution from India of £30,500,000, making together a total of £1,895,840,000. Or, if I follow the calculation of my right hon. friend of last year, who reckoned the Allied debt to us at half of its amount, loans to Allies, £834,225,000; loans to Dominions, £196,890,000; Indian contribution, £30,500,000, giving a total of £1,061,615,000. There will be—I cannot forget them (cheers)—in addition, the German indemnities (cheers), and so much of the remaining assets acquired out of vote of credit and arrears of existing excess profits duties still outstanding on the 1st of April next as is not required to meet the abnormal expenditure of that year caused by the overlapping of war conditions. The estimated balance of the vote of credit assets, as I have already stated, is £350,000,000, and the arrears of the existing excess profits duty £100,000,000.

I have now completed—and I thank the House for the patience with which they have heard me —(cheers) my immediate task. I have endeavoured to give the House as clear a picture as is yet possible both of our present position and of our future prospects. I have had to urge upon the House, as I may have to urge again and again, the necessity for severe economy in national and individual expenditure. I have no hope of any reduction in expenditure unless we in this House show an example. (Cheers.) I have had at the same time to impose further large burdens upon the community. I cannot hope that in the discharge of either part of my task I shall earn popularity. But in one point I find satisfaction. I am grateful that it has fallen to my lot to make the first proposal in this House for the statutory embodiment in our financial system of that policy of Imperial Preference with which my father's name and fame will be for ever linked. (Loud cheers.)

It is anticipated that in 1919 spirits will yield £52 m., beer £60 m., tea £14·2 m., sugar £39½ m., tobacco £46·8 m., motor spirit £8 m., matches £2·4 m., entertainments £8 m.

From the Chancellor's speech it will be seen that our present financial position is obscure, and the outlook uncertain. We are passing through the end of a great crisis which has necessitated an enormous emergency expenditure. We cannot forecast with any confidence our expenditure in the near future, the value of the salvage to be recovered in the process of clearing up after the War, or the times and amounts of repayment of debts due to us from other countries. The range of prices is another unknown factor. The heavy charge for naval and military pensions will gradually diminish, and much of the expenditure for reconstruction, like the land settlement and the provision of houses throughout the country, will be made once for all and will be productive of revenue. Our financial history for some years to come will be of absorbing interest and importance, and will deserve all the consideration which every one of us should give to it. No attempt is made here to enlarge upon the figures or the methods of our War Finance, or to touch upon currency, public credit and other difficult problems which the student cannot understand without special preparation. The near future is sure to see an abundance of financial literature of all kinds. A note is added on page 164 for the assistance of those who desire to pursue their studies further and to keep abreast of the subject.

APPENDIX

NOTE TO APPENDIX

IN using the figures in these tables allowance should be made for the growth of population and the rise of prices. On the 30th of June, 1907, the estimated population of the United Kingdom was about 43¾ m. It increased about 1 per cent. per annum till 1911, when the rate of increase fell to about ½ per cent., and since the War has remained at about a total of 48 m. The range of prices is measured by an Index Number. Taking that of the *Economist*, based upon forty-five principal commodities, and starting with an average of 100 for the five years 1901–1905, we have the following table:

End of July, 1914	..	116·6
,, December, 1914	..	127·3
,, ,, 1915	..	165·1
,, ,, 1916	..	223
,, ,, 1917	..	263·2
,, August, 1918	..	284·8 (highest war point reached).
,, November, 1918	..	282·6 (after the Armistice).
,, July, 1919	..	290·9

It may be noted that the tariff rates mentioned are the principal or governing rates. Beer, for example, pays a higher rate for each degree of gravity over 1055. Sugar is charged according to its quality as measured by the polariscope, and sugar of less than 98 degrees is taxed at a lower rate, but the great bulk of sugar imported is of 98 degrees or more. The minor changes in molasses, glucose, and saccharin which follow sugar are not specially mentioned. Tobacco is the unmanufactured leaf containing not less than 10 per cent. of moisture. The rates on cigars, cigarettes, snuff, tobacco with less than the standard amount of moisture, stripped leaf, etc., are not given here. Details will be found in such works of reference as *Whitaker's Almanack*, or more completely in the Annual Reports of the Commissioners of Customs and Excise and of the Commissioners of Inland Revenue. A summary of the tariff is included in the annual Statistical Abstract.

APPENDIX A.

AMOUNT OF THE IMPERIAL REVENUE AND EXPENDITURE OF THE UNITED KINGDOM, AND THE SURPLUS OR DEFICIENCY OF INCOME, IN EACH OF THE YEARS BEGINNING 1ST APRIL, 1907 TO 1918.

YEARS BEGINNING 1ST APRIL.	REVENUE. Receipts into the Exchequer.	EXPENDITURE. Issues out of the Exchequer (exclusive of Expenditure not chargeable against Revenue).	SURPLUS (+) or DEFICIENCY (−).
	£	£	£
1907	156,537,690	151,812,094	+ 4,725,596
1908	151,578,295	152,292,395	− 714,100
1909	131,696,456	157,944,611	}+ 5,606,766†
1910*	203,850,588	171,995,667	
1911	185,090,286	178,545,100	+ 6,545,186
1912	188,801,999	188,621,930	+ 180,069
1913	198,242,897	197,492,969	+ 749,928
1914	226,694,080	560,473,533	− 333,779,453
1915	336,766,825	1,559,158,377	− 1,222,391,552
1916	573,427,582	2,198,112,710	− 1,624,685,128
1917	707,234,565	2,696,221,405	− 1,988,986,840
1918	889,021,000	2,579,301,000	− 1,690,280,000

* Including arrears of 1909–10.

† The Revenue Act, 1911, directed that the income and expenditure of the years 1909–10 and 1910–11 should be aggregated for the purpose of determining the Old Sinking Fund for 1910–11.

AMOUNT OF THE IMPERIAL REVENUE (EXCHEQUER
PRINCIPAL HEADS THEREOF, IN EACH OF
(000's OMITTED.)

	1907	1908	1909	1910
	£	£	£	£
Customs	32,490	29,200	30,348	33,140
Excise	35,720	33,650	31,032	40,020
Estate, etc., Duties	19,070	18,370	21,766	25,452
Stamps (exclusive of Fee and Patent Stamps).	7,970	7,770	8,079	9,784
Land Tax	730	730	150	1,220
House Duty	1,960	1,900	560	3,080
Property and Income Tax (including Super Tax from 1910).*	32,380	33,930	13,295	61,946
Excess Profits Duty	—	—	—	—
Land Value Duties	—	—	—	520
Total	130,320	125,550	105,230	175,162
Postal Service .. · ..	17,880	17,770	18,220	19,220
Telegraph Service	} 4,420	{ 3,020	3,090	3,175
Telephone Service		1,510	1,720	1,955
Crown Lands (Net Receipts)	520	530	480	500
Receipts from Suez Canal Shares and Sundry Loans.	1,189	1,171	1,268	1,234
Miscellaneous:				
Fee and Patent Stamps ..	1,024	1,023	1,037	1,070
Receipts by Civil Departments, etc.	1,184	1,003	650	1,534
Total Miscellaneous ..	2,208	2,026	1,687	2,604
TOTAL REVENUE ..	156,537	151,578	131,696	203,850

* The rate in the £ was as follows:

	1907 and 1908.	1909 to 1913.
Nominal rate	1s.	1s. 2d.
Rate on Earned Income ..	9d.	9d. and 1s.
Rate of Super Tax ..	—	6d.

1 The rates for 1914 were doubled for the last four months of
2 The rates of Income Tax for 1915 were increased by 40 per
of Super Tax extended to 3s. 6d.

DIX B

1911	1912	1913	1914	1915	1916	1917	1918
£	£	£	£	£	£	£	£
33,649	33,485	35,450	38,662	59,606	70,561	71,261	102,780
38,380	38,000	39,590	42,313	61,210	56,380	38,772	59,440
25,392	25,248	27,359	28,382	31,035	31,232	31,674	30,262
9,454	10,059	9,966	7,577	6,764	7,878	8,300	12,438
750	700	700	630	660	640	665	630
2,130	2,000	2,000	1,930	1,990	1,940	1,960	1,850
44,804	44,806	47,249	69,399	128,320	205,033	239,509	291,486
—	—	—	—	140	139,920	220,214	285,028
481	455	715	412	363	521	685	664
155,040	154,753	163,029	189,305	290,088	514,105	613,040	784,758
19,650	20,300	21,190	20,400	24,100	24,350	25,200	29,400
3,105	3,100	3,080	3,000	3,350	3,350	3,500	3,800
2,945	5,775	6,530	6,250	6,450	6,400	6,600	6,800
530	530	530	545	550	650	690	760
1,281	1,418	1,579	1,276	2,431	8,055	6,156	11,680
1,031	1,066	1,078	961	943	934	934	—
1,507	1,859	1,225	4,956	8,853	15,582	51,214	—
2,538	2,925	2,303	5,917	9,796	16,516	52,148	52,303
185,090	188,801	198,242	226,694	336,766	573,427	707,234	889,021

1914.[1]	1915.[2]	1916 and 1917	1918.
1s. 3d.	2s. 6d.	5s.	6s.
9d. to 1s. 3d.	1s. 6d. to 2s. 6d.	2s. 3d. to 5s.	2s. 3d. to 6s.
5d. to 1s. 4d.	10d. to 2s. 8d.	10d. to 3s. 6d.	1s. to 4s. 6d.

the Income Tax year.
cent. for the second half of the Income Tax year and the scale

AMOUNT OF THE IMPERIAL EXPENDITURE (EX
THE PRINCIPAL HEADS THEREOF, IN EACH
(000's OMITTED.)

	1907	1908	1909	1910
I.—CONSOLIDATED FUND SERVICES:	£	£	£	£
National Debt Services:				
Inside the Permanent or Fixed Annual Charge:				
Interest of Funded Debt	15,773	15,652	15,490	15,377
Terminable Annuities ..	3,596	3,550	3,526	3,481
Interest of Unfunded Debt.	1,584	1,166	1,567	1,353
Management of the Debt.	180	175	173	175
New Sinking Fund ..	8,365	7,455	1,000	4,112
Total	29,500	28,000	21,757	24,500
Outside the Permanent or Fixed Annual Charge.	—	—	—	54
Total National Debt Services	29,500	28,000	21,757	24,554
Development Fund	—	—	—	500
Road Improvement Fund ..	—	—	—	862
Payments to Local Taxation Accounts, etc.	11,155	*9,824	9,445	9,881
Other Consolidated Fund Services:				
Civil List	470	470	470	470
Annuities and Pensions	284	271	265	299
Salaries and Allowances	77	77	72	56
Courts of Justice ..	515	518	518	514
Miscellaneous Services ..	624	331	327	323
Total	1,971	1,669	1,653	1,664
Total Consolidated Fund Services (carried forward)	42,627	39,493	32,856	37,462

* From 1st January, 1909, the collection of Dog, Gun, Game,
ferred to the Local Authorities.
† Interest, etc., on debt created under the War Loan Acts,

DIX C

1911	1912	1913	1914	1915	1916	1917	1918
£	£	£	£	£	£	£	£
15,202	15,000	14,787	14,632	12,934	7,965	7,953	7,949
3,517	3,540	3,202	2,931	2,897	2,860	2,809	2,573
1,158	1,171	1,115	1,771	4,330	8,630	8,519	12,403
173	166	166	162	175	327	547	713
4,447	4,620	5,228	1,000	—	—	—	—
24,500	24,500	24,500	20,497	20,338	19,782	19,828	23,638
—	—	—	†2,171	†39,911	†107,467	†170,023	†246,327
24,500	24,500	24,500	22,668	60,249	127,250	189,850	269,965
500	—	—	—	—	—	—	—
1,209	1,172	1,394	1,528	694	—	—	—
9,636	9,653	9,734	9,529	9,756	9,895	9,730	9,681
470	470	470	470	470	470	470	470
317	320	316	319	320	315	332	338
56	56	56	56	56	53	56	56
523	523	533	534	531	528	524	521
325	321	317	313	1,409	606	287	314
1,692	1,692	1,693	1,693	2,787	1,973	1,670	1,699
37,539	37,017	37,322	35,419	73,488	139,119	201,252	281,345

and Establishment Licences in England and Wales was trans-
1914 to 1918.

AMOUNT OF THE IMPERIAL EXPENDITURE (EX
THE PRINCIPAL HEADS THEREOF, IN EACH OF
(000's OMITTED.)

	1907	1908	1909	1910	1911
	£	£	£	£	£
Total Consolidated Fund Services — *Brought forward.*	42,627	39,493	32,856	37,462	37,539
II.					
SUPPLY SERVICES:					
Army	27,115	26,840	27,236	27,449	27,649
Ministry of Munitions	—	—	—	—	—
Navy	31,141	32,188	35,807	40,386	42,858
Air Force	—	—	—	—	—
Civil Services:					
I. Public Works and Buildings	2,692	2,872	3,113	3,167	3,217
II. Salaries and Expenses of Civil Departments.	2,916	2,875	3,041	3,366	4,144
III. Law and Justice	3,839	3,963	4,081	4,278	4,360
IV. Education, Science and Art.	17,359	17,369	17,907	18,744	18,983
V. Foreign and Colonial Services.	2,050	1,824	1,946	1,995	2,053
VI. { Non - effective and Charitable Services	817	778	891	801	804
{ Miscellaneous	507	587	535	949	681
VII. Old Age Pensions, Labour Exchanges, Insurance, etc.	—	2,070	8,496	9,798	11,759
Other Services.‡	—	—	—	—	—
Total Civil Services	30,180	32,338	40,010	43,098	46,001
Customs	947	974	*2,116	2,211	2,297
Inland Revenue	2,275	2,346	*1,226	1,708	1,654
Post Office Services	17,527	18,113	18,693	19,681	20,547
Total Supply Services	109,185	112,799	125,088	134,533	141,006
Votes of Credit—Naval and Military Operations, etc.	—	—	—	—	—
TOTAL EXPENDITURE chargeable against Revenue	151,812	152,292	157,944	171,995	178,545

* Excise transferred from Inland Revenue to Customs in
† Nominal amounts, the substantive issues being made
‡ Nominal amounts for Ministries of Pensions, Food,

(*Continued*)

CHEQUER ISSUES) OF THE UNITED KINGDOM, UNDER
THE YEARS BEGINNING 1st APRIL, 1907 to 1918

1912	1913	1914	1915	1916	1917	1918
£	£	£	£	£	£	£
37,017	37,322	35,419	73,488	139,119	201,252	281,345
28,071	28,346	28,885	†15	†15	†15	†15
—	—	—	†2	†1	†1	†1
44,365	48,833	51,550	†7	†17	†17	†17
—	—	—	—	—	—	†7
3,491	3,338	3,661	3,433	2,976	2,880	Figures not yet published
4,320	4,287	4,589	4,626	4,842	5,364	
4,470	4,491	4,755	4,664	4,474	4,791	
19,531	19,450	20,234	20,677	20,307	25,803	
2,151	1,523	1,838	1,497	1,229	1,317	
795	824	1,080	1,072	1,066	1,046	
509	322					
16,677	19,666	20,799	18,749	19,218	20,009	
—	—	—	—	1	32	
51,944	53,901	56,956	54,718	54,113	61,246	67,988
2,324	2,431	2,479	2,514	2,397	2,473	5,532
1,876	2,052	2,123	2,089	2,331	2,683	
23,024	24,607	26,060	26,673	26,454	25,738	26,396
151,604	160,170	168,053	86,018	85,328	92,169	99,956
—	—	357,000	1,399,652	1,973,664	2,402,800	2,198,000
188,621	197,492	560,473	1,559,158	2,198,112	2,696,221	2,579,301

1909.
under Votes of Credit.
Shipping, etc., and a grant to Lady Maude of £25,000 in 1917.

APPENDIX D.

TOTAL AMOUNT OF THE GROSS CAPITAL LIABILITIES OF THE STATE, THE ESTIMATED ASSETS, AND THE EXCHEQUER BALANCES ON 31st MARCH OF EACH YEAR FROM 1906 TO 1918. (000's OMITTED.)

At the close of the Financial Year ending 31st March.	Nominal Amount of Funded Debt. 1.	Estimated Capital Liability in respect of Terminable Annuities. 2.	Unfunded Debt. 3.	Totals of Columns 1 to 3. 4.	Other Capital Liabilities in Respect of Sums Borrowed under various Acts. 5.	Aggregate Gross Liabilities of the State as represented by the Total of Columns 4 and 5. 6.	Estimated Assets		Exchequer Balances at Banks of England and Ireland. 9.
							Suez Canal Shares. Estimated Market Value. 7.	Other Assets. 8.	
	£	£	£	£	£	£	£	£	£
1906	634,047	43,459	65,713	743,219	45,770	788,990	31,080	2,586	10,451
1907	631,928	40,864	56,713	729,505	49,659	779,164	31,796	4,272	6,932
1908	625,608	39,407	46,459	711,475	50,850	762,326	31,055	4,418	8,918
1909	621,838	38,009	42,839	702,687	51,433	754,121	32,667	4,493	6,350
1910	614,868	35,876	62,500	713,245	49,218	762,463	35,295	4,118	2,831
1911	610,315	34,417	40,500	685,232	47,840	733,072	37,608	4,003	13,546
1912	602,200	33,044	39,500	674,744	50,061	724,806	44,046	3,704	11,468
1913	593,453	31,519	36,500	661,473	54,814	716,288	39,015	3,707	6,329
1914	586,717	29,552	35,000	651,270	56,384	707,654	34,929	3,350	10,434
1915	583,290	28,040	497,486	1,108,817	56,984	1,165,801	29,993	3,242	83,450
1916	318,460	26,158	1,796,129	2,140,748	56,690	2,197,439	24,858	3,418	25,575
1917	317,787	24,045	3,669,613	4,011,445	52,199	4,063,644	27,464	3,216	26,435
1918	317,730	21,903	5,532,217	5,871,850	49,245	5,921,095	29,628	3,272	21,030

APPENDIX E.

COMPARISON OF PRINCIPAL CHANGES IN CUSTOMS AND EXCISE DUTIES, 1913 AND 1919.

	1913. £ s. d.		1919. £ s. d.
Beer, home-made, per 36 gallons of specific gravity of 1055.	0 7 9	..	2 10 0
Cinematograph films, imported, per foot of length:			
Blank	0 0 0	..	0 0 0½
Positives	0 0 0	..	0 0 1
Negatives	0 0 0	..	0 0 5
Clocks, watches, and parts thereof, imported.	0 0 0	..	One-third of value.
Cocoa, per cwt.	0 9 4	..	2 2 0
Coffee, roasted, per lb. ..	0 0 2	..	0 0 6
Dried fruit (other than currants), per cwt.	0 7 0	..	0 10 6
Matches, for every 10,000 (2d. extra on imported matches).	0 0 0	..	0 5 0
Mechanical lighters:			
Requiring the use of spirits.	0 0 0	..	0 1 0
Other sorts	0 0 0	..	0 0 6
Motor-cars, motor-cycles, and parts thereof, imported.	0 0 0	..	One-third of value.
Motor spirit, the gallon ..	0 0 3	..	0 0 6
Musical instruments imported	0 0 0	..	One-third of value.
*Spirits, imported, per gallon.	0 15 1	..	2 10 4
Home-made	0 14 9	..	1 10 0
Sugar exceeding 98 degrees of polarisation, per cwt.	0 1 10	..	1 5 8
Tea, per lb.	0 0 5	..	0 1 0
Tobacco, per lb.	0 3 8	..	0 8 2
Entertainments	0 0 0	..	From ½d. up to 2s. according to price of admission. After 15s. 6d. extra for every 5s. or part thereof.

* Additional rates are charged on spirits imported in bottle, immature spirits, and perfumed spirits.

APPENDIX F.

PRINCIPAL CHANGES IN TAXATION SINCE 1907.
(000's OMITTED.)

Year beginning 1st April,		Loss+ or Gain—to Revenue in a Full Year.*
		£
1908	Sugar duty reduced from 4s. 2d. to 1s. 10d. the cwt., with corresponding reductions in glucose, etc.	− 3,720
	Establishment licenses transferred to local authorities in England and Wales	− 1,650
	Stamp duty on certain marine insurances reduced from 3d. to 1d. per cent.	− 80
1909	New relief of tax on £10 for each child under 16 on incomes from £160 to £500	− 640
	Additional relief under Schedule A Income tax lands and houses	− 500
	Spirit duty increased from 11s. to 14s. 9d. per gallon on British and from 11s. 4d. to 15s. 1d. on foreign spirits (estimate for the year) ..	+ 1,600
	Tobacco duty increased from 3s. to 3s. 8d. per lb., with increases on cigars, manufactured and home-grown tobacco..	+ 2,600
	Motor spirit duty of 3d. per gallon imposed	+ 375

* Changes of taxation proposed in the Budget speech do not become effective until a later date. In some cases the estimate is given for the year in which the change took place; in others the Budget estimate for a complete year. Unless otherwise stated, the figure in this column is for a normal year as computed at the end of the year of change.

Year beginning 1st April,		Loss + or Gain − to Revenue in a Full Year.
		£
	Liquor licenses increased (estimate for the year)	+ 2,600
	Motor-car licenses increased (estimate for the year)	+ 260
	Death duties increased	+ 7,180
	Stamp duty increased on conveyances, leases, bearer securities, and contract notes	+ 1,290
	Income tax increased from 1s. to 1s. 2d.	+ 4,640
	Super tax imposed on incomes over £5,000—6d. in the £ on excess over £3,000	+ 2,500
	Abolition of abatements, etc., on income tax for non-residents in the United Kingdom	+ 220
	Land value duties imposed (estimate for the year)	+ 600
1910	No change.	
1911	,,	
1912	,,	
1913	,,	
1914	Relief from estate duty in respect of quick succession	− 156
	Income tax relief for each child increased from tax on £10 to tax on £20	− 220
	Additional relief for repairs, etc., of small houses	− 35
	Additional relief on incomes from £160 to £500	− 150
	Publicans' licences reduced for shortened hours (estimate for the year) ..	− 550
	Death duties increased	+ 5,400
	Income tax increased from 1s. 2d. to 1s. 3d.	+ 2,825
	Modified relief of earned income	+ 490
	Enlarged liability of income from investment abroad	+ 1,000
	Super tax extended to incomes of £3,000, and rates increased	+ 5,000

Year beginning 1st April,		Loss + or Gain − to Revenue in a Full Year.
		£
After declaration of War. 1915	Tea duty raised from 5d. to 8d. per lb. (estimate for the year)	+ 3,200
	Beer duty raised from 7s. 9d. to 25s. per barrel (estimate for the year) ..	+ 18,400
	Income tax rates doubled (estimate for the year)	+ 45,900
	Super tax rates doubled (estimate for the year)	+ 8,450
	Publicans' licences reduced for short-ened hours (estimate for the year) ..	− 200
	Income tax relief for each child increased from tax on £20 to tax on £25 (estimate for the year)	− 490
	Naval and military pay relieved of war increases for income tax in case of incomes not exceeding £300 (estimate for the year)	− 590
	Tea duty increased from 8d. to 1s. ..	+ 4,350
	Cocoa, coffee, etc., duties increased by one-half	+ 270
	Sugar duty raised from 1s. 10d. to 9s. 4d. per cwt. (estimate for the year)	+ 11,700
	Dried fruits (except currants): duty raised from 7s. to 10s. 6d. per cwt...	+ 120
	Tobacco duties increased by one-half ..	+ 8,250
	Motor spirit duty doubled (estimate for the year)	+ 850
	Patent medicine duty doubled.. ..	+ 260
	Motor-cars, motor-cycles, etc., imported: Customs duty of ⅓ of value..	+ 530
	Musical instruments imported: Customs duty of ⅓ of value	+ 40
	Clocks, watches, etc., imported: Customs duty of ⅓ of value	+ 220
	Cinematograph films imported: Customs duty imposed	+ 300
	Income tax increased by 40 per cent. ...	+ 37,650
	Exemption limit lowered from £160 to £130 and abatements reduced ..	+ 4,760
	Increased liability under Schedule B (farmers' profits)	+ 2,240

Year beginning 1st April,		Loss+ or Gain – to Revenue in a Full Year.*
		£
	Super tax increased on incomes over £8,000	+ 2,685
	Excess profit duty: 50 per cent. of excess over pre-war profits	+ 30,000
1916	Income tax increased to 5s. and scale altered	+ 43,500
	Sugar duty increased by ½d. per lb. ..	+ 7,000
	Cocoa, coffee, and chicory duties increased to £2 2s. per cwt.	+ 2,000
	Matches taxed 3s. 4d. for every 10,000	+ 2,000
	Table-waters taxed	+ 2,000
	Excess profits duty increased to 60 per cent.	+ 11,000
	Entertainment tax imposed	+ 5,000
	Motor-spirit licence duty increased ..	+ 800
1917	Tobacco duty increased by 1s. 10d. per lb.	+ 6,000
	Entertainments duty increased ..	+ 100
	Excess profits duty raised from 60 to 80 per cent.	+ 20,000
	Reduction of liquor licence duty in special cases	– 900
1918	Post Office rates increased	+ 4,000
	Cheque stamp duty raised from 1d. to 2d.	+ 1,000
	Income tax increased from 5s. to 6s. ... (Children allowance extended to wife, and limit of income for allowance raised to £800.)	+ 41,400
	Super tax increased	+ 5,300
	Spirit duty raised from 14s. 9d. to 30s. a gallon	+ 11,150
	Beer duty raised from 25s. to 50s. a barrel	+ 15,700
	Tobacco (unstripped and unmanufactured) duty increased from 6s. 5d. to 8s. 2d.	+ 8,000
	Matches duty increased by one-half ..	+ 600
	Sugar duty raised from 14s. to 25s. 8d. per cwt.	+ 13,200

* The figures on this page are Budget estimates only.

NOTE ON FURTHER READING

EVERYONE should read Adam Smith's *Wealth of Nations*, which is one of the great books of the world, and an excellent foundation for the study of finance. Professor Marshall's *Economics of Industry* and Professor J. S. Nicholson's *Elements of Economics* (for advanced students their *Principles*) will give a good grasp of economic reasoning. The only considerable British work on the general principles of finance is the *Public Finance* of Professor Bastable. I have attempted in my *Financial System of the United Kingdom* to explain the mechanism and formal procedure of British finance, and in *National Economy* to outline the art of financial administration. Lieut.-Commander Hilton Young, M.P., describes *Our Financial System* in a popular form. *Our Money and the State* and other writings by Mr. Hartley Withers will be found useful.

For the technical side of statistics and for their practical handling the works of Dr. Bowley and Sir R. Giffen may be referred to. For local taxation and finance Professor S. J. Chapman's *Local Government and State Aid*.

If it is desired to make a special study of a particular portion of the subject of finance, such as Customs, Death-Duties, Excise, Income Tax, Debt, etc., the reader will find under the appropriate articles in such works of reference as the *Encyclopædia Britannica* or Palgrave's *Dictionary of Political Economy* a list of the principal authorities, and as each authority refers to a great many others the line of inquiry may be easily followed. Mention may, however, be made of Dowell's *History of Taxes and Taxation,* and of the historical accounts of *British Budgets* in Sir B. Mallet's volume of that name, in Sir S. Northcote's *Twenty Years of Financial Policy*, and Lord Buxton's *Finance and Politics*. There is nothing like a study of the actual budgets to bring us to grips with the realities of finance.

The *Introduction to the Study of Finance* by an American Professor, C. C. Plehn, can be recommended to beginners. Many foreign works, like those of Adolph Wagner, P. Leroy Beaulieu, and N. C. Pierson, and the writings of American authorities like Professor E. R. A. Seligman and H. C. Adams, are of great value. But by the time the reader is able to make use of works of this kind he will have passed beyond the stage for which this primer is designed.

INDEX